How to be a

BOURBON
BADASS ™

How to be a
BOURBON
BADASS ™

LINDA RUFFENACH

PHOTOGRAPHY BY ERIN TRIMBLE

This book is a publication of
RED LIGHTNING BOOKS
1320 East 10th Street | Bloomington, Indiana 47405 USA
redlightningbooks.com

Manufactured in the United States of America

ISBN 978-1-68435-008-7 (cloth)
ISBN 978-1-68435-009-4 (ebook)

5 6 27 26 25 24 23 22

This book is dedicated to all of the badass women out there who have broken through barriers to empower other women to achieve greatness. Especially my mom, who in my mind will always be the first badass in my life.

And to my fabulous husband, Fred. You are the one who reignited my passion for bourbon. You have been my best friend, my partner, and my biggest cheerleader every step of this journey.

Contents

Foreword

Pamela Heilmann
Master Distiller, Vice President of Production
MICHTER'S DISTILLERY, LLC

It may have been a fluke that led me to my start in the distillery business, but a passion and respect for the challenging process and an industry with an immense heritage kept me in it. My journey has been rewarding and inspiring. One of my mentors once said to me, "In the distilling industry, you learn something new every day, and if you don't think so you shouldn't be in the business." He was a veteran distillery operator and one of the many teachers I've had in my career. It was some of the best advice I've ever been given. If you close your mind to learning from anyone and everyone, you can't grow. I don't pretend to know all there is to know about making bourbon/whiskey . . . that is for sure! What I can tell you is that I learn something new every day from, at times, the most unlikely sources.

Prior to joining Michter's, I didn't have any interaction with the consumers who enjoyed the products we made. I was always behind the scenes at the production plant. My first foray into interacting with consumers was as a distiller for Michter's Distillery at a 2014 tasting. It was hosted at Westport Whiskey & Wine in Louisville, Kentucky, by Chris Zaborowski in partnership with an organization known as Whisky Chicks, led by founder Linda Ruffenach. I was very nervous. It was my first time talking in front of a crowd about what I did every day. I thought, *What will I be able to say to these women that would interest them?* As it turned out, it was a most memorable and enjoyable experience. I found a diverse group of women from all backgrounds and walks of life who were bonding over a common interest: bourbon/whiskey. They were there to learn and enjoy. They were warm, excited, and engaged. They were having fun! In turn, I had fun and enjoyed talking to them and sharing my experiences. They made my first-ever tasting very comfortable, and the evening flew by. Linda and Chris created an environment that allowed people to comfortably be themselves while exposing them to different whiskeys.

Having been involved in many tastings with Michter's since that first one, I recently had the pleasure of leading a large tasting of about a hundred people, including both new and established consumers. I like to make sure that everyone at a tasting has a great experience. It is about exposing the consumer to our products in a comfortable and enjoyable way. Prior to the start of the tasting, I was conversing with a woman who was participating in her first bourbon tasting. She doubted that she could identify any particular flavors in what she was tasting. We discussed relating what you smell and taste to other things in your life. Everyday events, such as cooking and eating out, and your environment all contribute to how you identify what you taste and smell when you drink whiskey. We all tasted, and then I asked the crowd to tell me what they experienced. I watched her as people in the crowd were yelling out their answers. She had a funny expression on her face. I asked her (off the microphone) if she had experienced something different that she would like to share. She said, "Well I get a nutty taste—like almonds. Weird?" I told her that was great and few people get that nutty characteristic when they taste our bourbon. This interaction and many like this are what keep me excited and engaged to share our whiskeys with all consumers.

I had an experience many years ago, while participating in a tasting, when the person leading indicated the flavors and aromas we should be identifying. I remember thinking that I must not be very good at this because I didn't experience or identify all the same things he did. I am not a fan of telling people what they should experience. I always share my opinion last, rather than sway consumers' experiences with my opinion. There are so many unique palates out there, and a tasting for me is all about what we as individuals taste. There is no right or wrong answer. It is simply what you taste and what you like.

My first experience leading, at the tasting with Linda and the Whisky Chicks, proved to be a great one as they were awesome facilitators for this learning experience. So whether you are beginning your journey or started some time ago, please keep your mind open to learning something new every day about this great industry and process.

Pamela Heilmann

Introduction

I believe all of us have an inner badass. We need to give ourselves permission to let it show. I have discovered that possessing knowledge and confidence about bourbon and whiskey can provide you with the self-assurance to let your inner badass shine through. Particularly for women, breaking away from conventional wisdom that whiskey is a man's drink further empowers us to knock down other perceived barriers.

I do not consider myself an expert on bourbon. Instead, I am an expert on my own bourbon journey. My wish for you is that *you* become an expert on *your* journey. In writing this book, I spoke with many of the experts and rock stars of the industry. They shared highlights from their personal journeys and the stories that helped ignite their passion for the amber spirit we call bourbon.

Some of their stories begin a little rough—with experiences from college that involved a little too much of the brown stuff. For others their stories begin much like mine, with the smell of bourbon taking them back to family gatherings and celebrations. No matter whether you are a beer drinker, a wine drinker, or a lover of cosmopolitans, I believe you can discover something to love about bourbon. It may be in a cocktail, straight up, on the rocks, or with a splash of soda. You will never know until you give it a try.

I hope this book will make your journey to becoming a Bourbon Badass easy and enjoyable. If you only take one thing away from this book, let it be that there is no right way or wrong way to drink bourbon. The only way that matters is your way!

Linda Ruffenach

How to be a

BOURBON
BADASS ™

The Journey Begins

ONE | *The Journey Begins*

Not until I was older did I realize what an amazing privilege it was to grow up in the heart of bourbon country. Going for a Sunday drive through the winding roads and rolling hills of Kentucky's backcountry is magical. It remains one of my favorite childhood memories. My parents, sister, two brothers, and I would pile into our baby blue 1963 Chevy Nova station wagon and set off for our next big adventure. As the youngest, I had to strain to get a glimpse of the graceful thoroughbreds lazily grazing in fields of bluegrass. I can still smell the scent of tobacco drying in open barns and the sweet aroma of corn mash wafting from the aging warehouses that dotted the countryside. This was home to me. Little did I know that years later I would once again travel those same backroads to discover and explore the magic of Kentucky bourbon.

When I was younger and we were celebrating a birthday or special occasion, my dad's parents, Pepaw and Memaw, would take us to the Melrose Inn in Prospect, Kentucky. It was just a few miles outside downtown Louisville, but for a child it was a destination. The Melrose meant fresh-baked yeast rolls, tangy corn relish, and the sweet flavor of spice cake with bourbon caramel frosting or, if we were really lucky, a piece of Kern's Kitchen's famous Derby-Pie®. Of course, on our way out there, we had to stop at a roadside "package shop" to buy a pint of bourbon, since Prospect was in a dry county. We settled into the private family dining room, where set-ups for cocktails awaited us. Well, not for the kids, but for the adults. I watched in fascination as my regal grandfather meticulously measured the shots and carefully balanced the portions of whiskey, soda, and ice for the perfect Bourbon Highball. It's no wonder I developed a taste for that caramel brown elixir and a love for all things Kentucky.

The truth is, my bourbon-tasting days started early. My oldest brother, Rob, loves to tell this story. On a Christmas Eve when I was just a few years old, my parents were entertaining in the basement, and just like every Christmas Eve, they were making frozen Whiskey Sours for the crowd of family, friends, and neighbors. They were too busy to notice the little girl in footie pajamas with a natural curiosity and a knack for getting into trouble. I spotted that bright red maraschino cherry on top of that sweet frozen concoction, and before anyone noticed, I had downed the entire drink. Rob told on me, the family panicked, but I managed to survive. I have no memory of the incident. Perhaps I was too young. Perhaps the bourbon had something to do with it. To this day, bourbon will always be connected with family, friends, and celebration.

Everyone's journey with whiskey and bourbon is different. For me, bourbon conjures up pleasant memories from my childhood: Making bourbon balls with my favorite aunt. My mother soothing our scratchy throats with a shot of Yukon Jack. From the basement steps, watching my parents prepare for the party I was not invited to attend but so wanted to be a part of. For others, it brings back not-so-nice flashbacks of a night of overindulgence in college. Still others may see whiskey and bourbon as too intimidating to even consider as a drink option. When I created the Whisky

My dad's parents (a.k.a. Memaw and Pepaw) always enjoyed Kentucky bourbon.

The Melrose Inn was one of our favorite places for family celebrations when I was a kid.

Left to right: I am around two or three in this photo with my brothers, Rob and Mike, and sister, Anna.

Chicks, I simply wanted to meet other women over a topic other than job, spouse, or kids. It has evolved into a warm and welcoming place where women of drinking age, from their early twenties to their nineties and from diverse backgrounds and experiences, can come together to savor the depth and complexity that a good glass of bourbon can contain. It's where the novice, the enthusiast, and the connoisseur can learn from each other and enjoy the pleasures of life.

I have been very fortunate to accompany many women on their journey with bourbon and whiskey. Watching others take their first sip of bourbon has taught me several things, the first of which is don't start with a straight shot of bourbon or it may be your last. If you are a red wine drinker, chances are you did not start out drinking a heavy zinfandel. You probably started with something much sweeter and lighter. Over time you probably began to venture into bigger, bolder flavors. Even if you like cabernet, you probably don't like every cabernet you taste. Your palate may prefer a sweet wine over a dry wine. Your tastes and preferences about wine will also change over time and can be influenced by what you are eating, the time of the year, or the occasion. Your journey with bourbon will be similar. That is part of the adventure.

As you might have done with wine, I suggest you try lots of different bourbons until you find the characteristics you like. Spirits with almost the exact same ingredients can taste dramatically different, sometimes in bold ways, sometimes in subtle ways. The great news for whiskey novices and explorers is that an increasing number of boutique and chain liquor stores have tasting rooms, not just for wine but also for bourbons and whiskies. A good bourbon purveyor will guide you beyond the old standards, like Maker's Mark, Jim Beam, or Jack Daniels (which technically is not bourbon but Tennessee whiskey instead).

Adults-Only Make-Ahead Frozen Whiskey Sours

Ingredients: frozen lemonade concentrate, frozen orange juice concentrate, water, bourbon, maraschino cherry, and orange slices

Directions: In a large container, mix together one 6-ounce can frozen lemonade concentrate with one 6-ounce can frozen orange juice concentrate. Add 3 cups of water and 1 ½ cups of bourbon. Freeze overnight. Scoop into glasses and top with a maraschino cherry and an orange slice.

Pepaw's Perfect Bourbon Highball

Fill a tall narrow-mouthed 12-ounce glass with ice. Add 2 ounces of Very Old Barton Bourbon and top with Canada Mist Ginger Ale. Stir and enjoy!

In most metropolitan areas, a Google search will lead you to at least a few restaurants that offer extensive whiskey selections. Some may even offer bourbon "flights," which are a way to taste a variety of small samples for a nominal cost. Your best bet is a good bartender who already knows his or her bourbon and will walk you through your first pioneering steps into bourbon country.

Living in Louisville, Kentucky, I'm fortunate to have a wide variety of distilleries within driving distance—a good reason to visit the Derby City. Much of my passion and knowledge about bourbon can be attributed to Chris Zaborowski, the owner and proprietor of the Louisville-based Westport Whiskey & Wine. Chris has been a tour guide for many on their whiskey journey. Perhaps the reason he is so good at his craft is that, like many of us, he started with wine. He dedicated many years to learning and teaching about the wine industry. It all started when he was working for a liquor store and asked to take a class on wine. Two years later Chris was teaching the class. He was the first in Kentucky to be recognized as a certified wine specialist by the Society of Wine Educators.

Chris has spent most of his career in the wholesale spirits business. He began his bourbon journey in the late '90s. The distribution company where he worked as vice president of sales and marketing had just acquired Jim Beam as a client. He was asked to visit the distillery and get to know their products. That is where he met and toured with master distiller Jerry Dalton, assistant distiller Pam Heilmann, and the infamous Booker Noe. Chris was awed by the many steps it took to make a single bottle of bourbon. The attention to detail required at every stage, from milling the grains to getting

Chris Zaborowski carefully selecting a single barrel from Wild Turkey.

the label exactly right on a completed bottle of Booker Noe, was fascinating. The distillers were seeing, doing, and tasting at all stages. Chris was hooked.

In 2008, he and a group of business partners decided to open their own liquor store. The bourbon boom had not yet hit. They purposely named their new venture Westport Whiskey & Wine because they felt that both the whiskey and the wine markets were underserved. They wanted Westport to be recognized for having the best selection in Kentucky, and they were willing to span the globe to make that happen. Chris personally researched products from other areas and made alliances with distributors to find selections that were not available in Kentucky. Sometimes Westport Whiskey & Wine was the only place in the state to buy a specific bottle, even if they only carried a case or two.

When Chris and his partners designed their store, they included a tasting room, because in Chris's opinion, the best way to learn about a product is to try it. Their current tasting room has over 250 bourbons and whiskies from all over the world. Westport has opened the eyes of many to the complexities and enjoyment of whiskies and wines. Chris's wife, Robin Zaborowski, is one of the many.

Robin, like many women, was not at all interested in drinking bourbon. She had tried it and just did not like it. She liked her vodka tonics and the occasional glass of wine, especially if it was a good robust wine. One evening, Chris needed Robin to help out at the store hosting a new product introduction and tasting by Maker's Mark. There,

Robin met Kevin Smith, who convinced her to try a lab sample of their new bourbon. One sip and she fell in love. It was not what she expected at all. She kept texting Chris about her new discovery. She couldn't get over her amazement that she actually liked bourbon! That product was Maker's 46. And these days there is always a bottle handy in the Zaborowskis' liquor cabinet. To this day, Maker's Mark owner Bill Samuels credits Robin's enthusiasm for helping boost sales of Maker's 46.

When I talk about Whisky Chicks, people naturally want to know my favorite bourbon. I have two boys, and it's just like asking someone to pick their favorite child: it's impossible to pick a favorite bourbon. I enjoy different bourbons for different reasons, seasons, and occasions. Your own individual taste preferences and where you are in your exploration will influence your selection. I asked my bourbon mentor, Chris, to help me put together a few suggestions. He reminded me that your current preferences can be a guide to determining which bourbons you prefer.

A white wine drinker is probably not going to appreciate big, bold, robust flavors the same way a red wine drinker would. They may prefer a less potent entry point like 86 proof Old Forester, which is sweet, soft, and easy to drink. Red wine drinkers may like a 100 proof with a higher rye content like Old Grand-Dad Bonded Bourbon. If you prefer an even sweeter wine or cocktail, Basil Hayden's is another a great place to start.

The well-informed beginner and connoisseur bourbon drinkers both know one thing: no one can tell you what you like or don't like. You are empowered to drink bourbon the way that you want to drink bourbon. As Colleen Thomas, a good friend and bourbon ambassador for the Kentucky Distillers' Association, puts it, "If you like Pappy's and Dr. Pepper, then drink Pappy's and Dr. Pepper." More about Pappy's later (see page 78). Let's just say it would be like drinking Dom Perignon champagne with nachos. Hey, I'm not judging. It just depends on what you like.

Chris Zaborowski with his wife, Robin.

Starting Lineup for the

Novice Bourbon Drinker

You have to start somewhere, so why not start with bourbons that are easy to find and that highlight the subtle differences between proof, mash bill, and style? The recommended tasting order is based on style then proof. Finishing with Maker's Mark allows you to compare bourbons where rye is the secondary grain versus wheat.

Basil Hayden's is produced by Jim Beam and is the perfect bourbon for starting your bourbon journey. At only 80 proof, it has a smooth start and finish. Made from 63 percent corn, 27 percent rye, and 10 percent barley, it is considered a high rye and will have a slightly peppery flavor mixed with a hint of honey, citrus, and peppermint. The flavors are very subtle and not overpowering, and because of this it is more of a sipping bourbon than one for cocktails. It is perfect over ice.

Bulleit Bourbon is one of my personal favorites. When I go out and want to opt for something familiar, Bulleit on the rocks is my go-to bourbon. It makes a great Old Fashioned, and the Bulleit Rye is amazing in a Manhattan. A 90 proof bourbon made from 68 percent corn, 28 percent rye, and 4 percent malted barley, it has a beautiful amber color that hits the mid-palate just perfectly with hints of baking spice, toffee, and maple with a balanced finish.

Woodford Reserve Kentucky Straight Bourbon, at 90.4 proof, is considered an everyday bourbon by many. It is incredibly versatile, working well in cocktails, savory and sweet dishes, on the rocks, and neat. One whiff of the nose and you pick up caramel with bits of mint and orange mixed with dried fruit and vanilla. The first taste brings out the citrus and cocoa. This is one you want to try with different foods, such as chocolate, nuts, or a hard cheese. It is an amazing experience that changes the flavor and highlights the strength and versatility of this bourbon.

1792 Small Batch is made in Bardstown, Kentucky, by the Barton 1792 distillery using the same mash bill—75 percent corn, 15 percent rye, and 10 percent barley—as the Very Old Barton brand, which is probably why I like it so much. Very Old Barton was what we always kept under the kitchen sink ready for company when I was a child. On Friday nights, I like to drink the modern-day version over ice with a bonfire going in the backyard. It pairs incredibly well with the melted chocolate and toasted marshmallow of a s'more. The aroma of caramel and dark fruits is the first thing I notice, with just a hint of baking spice. Flavors of maple and caramel come through on the palate, and the 93.7 proof whiskey finishes smooth.

Maker's Mark is one of the most recognizable bourbons, with its square bottle and distinctive red wax seal. The bourbon itself is 90 proof and is 70 percent corn, 16 percent wheat, and 14 percent malted barley. It is said that during the process of creating the recipe for Maker's Mark, the founder, Bill Samuels, had his wife bake up loaves of bread using different mixes of grain. In his opinion, the one without rye was the best. This 90 proof bourbon has a much sweeter finish than one made with the traditional rye. There are hints of vanilla and caramel that add an extra lusciousness to each sip. Many people start with Maker's and Coke or Maker's and ginger ale and work their way to Maker's and water, eventually drinking it neat or on the rocks. This is a great bourbon to cook with.

Lineup for the
Enthusiastic Learner

When you are ready to up your game and venture into
other bourbons, here are a few to try. The recommended order
is to try them from lowest to highest proof.

Four Roses Small Batch, at 90 proof, combines the best of their proprietary blends together at just the right time to create one of the smoothest bourbons around. With just the right amount of spice and sweet, fruity flavors, it is soon to become a favorite. The nose starts off with a bit of spice, fruit, and vanilla. When it hits your palate, you first notice the rich, creamy feel that livens up your palate with sweet berries and caramel. The soft, smooth finish is my favorite part.

Jefferson's Reserve Very Old Kentucky Straight Bourbon Small Batch says it all. The special blend of bourbon marries together three different bourbons, some aged up to twenty years, to create an amazing flavor profile that does not disappoint. They only blend together eight to twelve casks, and the bourbon is brought down to 90 proof using Kentucky limestone water. The nose is full of creamy vanilla, sweet spice, and dried fruits. On the tongue, you can detect notes of tobacco, corn, and toffee. The finish is soft and dry.

Michter's US 1 Kentucky Straight Bourbon is one of my all-time favorite small batch bourbons, coming in at 91.4 proof. While there is no legal definition for "small batch," Michter's never pulls more than a couple dozen barrels into a bottling run, as compared to other small batch brands on the market who might blend together a few thousand barrels. When pouring a sample, I am hit with the sweet smells of a rick house and can detect notes of vanilla, tobacco, and cinnamon. It starts off sweet with a bit of pepper on the back end. The finish is smooth and does not disappoint with flavors of caramel, vanilla, and apricots. My favorite way to drink this one is either neat or over ice.

Larceny is produced by Heaven Hill Distillery, the largest independent, family-owned producer and marketer of distilled spirits in the United States. While there is no age statement on the packaging, this bourbon has been hand selected by the master distillers to have a taste profile of a six-year bourbon. Its mash bill of 75 percent corn, 20 percent wheat, and 5 percent malted barley delivers a smooth tasting 92 proof bourbon. The wheat comes through on the nose with hints of fresh-baked bread with warm honey butter. The richness of the bourbon shows through on the first taste, delivering hints of caramel and honey.

Blanton's Original Single Barrel has very distinctive packaging that makes an impressive addition to any bar, but it is what's inside that will impress your friends. Billed as the world's first modern single barrel bourbon, Blanton's is hand selected from Warehouse H at Buffalo Trace. This 93 proof spirit starts out with an aroma of nuts, vanilla, and chocolate with hints of citrus. It fills the palate with brown sugar and orange cloves and finishes with a bit of honey and orange. This versatile bourbon is equally amazing straight on the rocks or in a cocktail.

Lineup for the
Connoisseur

These are some of my favorite higher-end bourbons for you to try
when you are ready to take your journey to the next level.

Evan Williams Single Barrel Vintage
is an 86.6 proof bourbon that is hand
selected by the master distiller and marked
with the vintage date it was put into oak,
along with the year it was bottled and the
exact serial number of the single barrel
that the bourbon was drawn from. Because
they come from different barrels, each
bottle is uniquely different yet similar. You
will find common elements of dark caramel
nose combined with charred oak. On your
palate, you will generally find a little spice
combined apple and citrus.

**Angel's Envy Kentucky Straight
Bourbon** is finished in port wine casks,
leaving it with a delicious richness. The
bourbon is aged for up to six years and
carefully blended into a small batch of
eight to twelve barrels. Each barrel will lose
about 5 percent of the spirit to evaporation,
or "the Angel's Share." The story is that
what's left behind is truly worthy of envy.
The bourbon is then finished for three to
six months in the ruby port wine casks to
further enhance the bourbon. The nose
presents subtle aromas of vanilla, dried
fruits, toasted nuts, and a hint of maple.
The first taste is of vanilla, ripe fruits, and
a hint of maple and bitter chocolate. The
finish is where you capture the subtleness of
the port wine casks with a bit of sweetness
lingering on the palate.

**Blade & Bow 22-Year-Old Kentucky
Straight Bourbon Whiskey** is a
very limited one-time release of twenty-
two-year-old bourbon whiskey distilled at
both the Bernheim distillery in Louisville
(now Heaven Hill) and the Buffalo Trace
distillery in Frankfort. This 92 proof bourbon

is incredibly smooth with hints of baked
apples, honey, and brown sugar. The nose
has strong notes of vanilla, caramel, and fig.
The finish has a spice that lingers for a bit
but is not overpowering, allowing the flavors
of vanilla and caramel to come through.

Russell's Reserve Single Barrel is
aged in barrels handpicked by the master
distillers at Wild Turkey. They look for
the deepest No. 4 "alligator" char on the
American White Oak barrels. Each barrel
is bottled at 110 proof. To guarantee
maximum flavor, this particular bourbon
does not go through the traditional chilled
filtration. Chilled filtration is used just before
bottling to remove anything left in the
whiskey. A nonfiltered whiskey that is 46
percent ABV or lower will go cloudy when
water or ice is added and when the whiskey
is cooled. Each barrel has its own unique
personality, but most will have the Wild
Turkey signature rich toffee and vanilla taste.

Old Forester 1870 Original Batch
echoes George Garvin Brown's original 1870
batching process. Back then, Brown batched
barrels obtained from three distilleries to
create a consistent flavor profile. To emulate
that process, barrels are selected from three
warehouses, each barrel originating from a
different day of production, with a different
entry proof and a different age profile. The
three expressions of Old Forester are then
batched together to craft Old Forester
1870 Original Batch. The nose carries
strong scents of baking spice mixed with
citrus fruits. The aroma translates into the
flavor experience with the added luxury of
shortbread. The finish is soft with a bit of the
fruit and spice lingering.

Chocolate Bourbon Pecan Pie

Not quite the same as the official Derby-Pie but a delicious substitute. Featuring pottery from another local favorite, Stoneware & Co.

The Melrose Inn is not only a place full of family memories; it is also home to the famous Kern's Kitchen Derby-Pie. Created over half a century ago, the chocolate, bourbon-infused walnut pie was developed by George Kern with the help of his parents, Walter and Leaudra. By 1968, Derby-Pie had become so successful that the name was registered with the US Patent Office and the Commonwealth of Kentucky. Since then it has been baked and distributed solely by Kern's Kitchen, a small family operation owned by the Kerns' grandson, Alan Rupp. The recipe is a secret, known only to a small group of Kern family members and a single Kern's Kitchen employee (who actually mixes the recipe today).

There is nothing quite like the original Derby-Pie, but the recipe is top secret and not something you can repeat at home. When we cannot find the original at the store, the following recipe is a variation we serve at family gatherings. The simplicity of the recipe makes it easy to pull together at the last minute for an impressive dessert at your next gathering.

Chocolate Bourbon Pecan Pie

SERVES 8

Ingredients:

1 stick softened butter

1 cup sugar

2 eggs, beaten

½ cup flour

a pinch of salt

2 tablespoons Kentucky bourbon*

1 teaspoon vanilla

1 cup chocolate chips

1 cup chopped pecans

Cream butter and sugar, then add eggs, flour, salt, bourbon, and vanilla. Mix until combined. Fold in chocolate chips and pecans. Pour into a partially baked pie shell, and bake at 350° for 30–40 minutes until center is set. Serve warm or at room temperature.

If you want more bourbon flavor, use 3 tablespoons bourbon and skip the vanilla.

Bourbon Basics

TWO | *Bourbon Basics*

When you think of a bourbon drinker, what pictures come to mind? A captain of industry lounging in a smoky drawing room, sipping his brown drink out of heavy lead crystal? Perhaps it's a John Wayne–type bellying up to the bar and asking for a shot of whiskey neat. How many imagine a ninety-four-year-old great-grandmother or a stay-at-home mom? Honestly, it could be any of them because all that is required to be a bourbon drinker is a passion for bourbon. Admittedly, I have not always had that passion. In fact, it was my husband, Fred, a native of Philadelphia, who brought me back home to my Kentucky bourbon roots. When he moved to Louisville, he insisted on finding out why this caramel elixir appealed to so many. I still laugh at his reaction the first time he tried bourbon. He took a big swig and nearly spit it out across the room. For this classic gin-and-tonic guy, the heavy oak flavor and high alcohol content overwhelmed his senses. It was not a pleasant experience. But as a transplant now living in the heart of bourbon country, he felt it was his duty to learn more about this native spirit and better understand its widespread popularity. His natural curiosity and his love of food, wine, and spirits reignited my own passion for this Kentucky favorite.

Fred is a researcher, so when he is passionate about something, you better believe he is going to learn every nuance and detail of it. Initially, Fred soaked up all he could discover about bourbon, from how it is made to the fascinating history of the founding families. Over time, he has familiarized himself with the major players in the industry, touring distilleries and joining a local organization called the Bourbon Society. I rode his coattails right into my first Bourbon Society event. It was a pivotal experience. The event was held at the Pendennis Club, an old private gentlemen's club in Louisville, renowned as the home of the Old Fashioned cocktail. The Bourbon Society was celebrating the anniversary of Repeal Day.

Pendennis Old Fashioned

Ingredients: sugar, Angostura bitters, water, bourbon, and orange rind

Muddle together in a glass 1 teaspoon sugar and 2 dashes Angostura bitters. Add 1 teaspoon water to dissolve sugar. Add 2 ounces Kentucky bourbon and ice, and stir. Twist a piece of orange rind in the glass and swipe around rim of glass before serving.

Like most of the women at the event, I was there with my husband. I knew little about bourbon and proceeded to blindly taste and sample the selections available. At home, Fred was gathering quite a collection of bourbons. It was becoming a hot topic in town, and through osmosis, I was becoming more aware of the number of distilleries and the amount of bourbon produced in my home state. People from around the world were becoming fascinated with bourbon and the rock stars who were producing it. All I knew about bourbon was that once a year, my parents would buy a bottle of Very Old Barton. It was so big it required its own handle to pour at our family events. In more recent years, it has been replaced by a bottle of Woodford Reserve. That night at the Pendennis Club, I was about to get my first real lesson in bourbon.

At the party, I struck up a conversation with a very nice older couple from Lawrenceburg, Kentucky. We talked about their hometown. I learned they had been together since they were teenagers. You could see that they had an amazing love and admiration for each other. Even in casual conversation they flirted and teased. The wife blushed with delight every time her husband shared a special memory about their life together, which he delivered with a mischievous sparkle in his eye. He was witty, telling funny stories about living in a small town. He apparently had been part of a family-owned business and spoke with pride about working alongside his children.

When our conversation fell into a lull, I politely excused myself. I couldn't wait to tell Fred about this fascinating couple I had met. Fred quickly asked me if I knew who I had been talking to. "Of course," I replied, "Jimmy and his wife, Joretta." My husband proceeded to inform me that Jimmy was Jimmy Russell. Okay . . . I asked, "Who is that?" Turned out, Jimmy Russell is the master distiller for Wild Turkey. An icon in the world of bourbon, he is considered by many to be one of the industry's leading pioneers and experts on all things bourbon. To quote Kentucky Distillers' Association president Eric Gregory, "If there was a Mount Rushmore of Bourbon, Jimmy Russell would be one of the first faces on it." I was smitten by his humble demeanor, his unassuming character, and his warmth. That describes many of the prominent figures in this industry. The people are genuine, collaborative, and approachable. It doesn't matter if they are meeting you for the first time or the fiftieth. They treat you like a long-lost relative, welcoming you with open arms. Kind of like bourbon itself.

That same evening, I met another incredible woman who was also a member of the Bourbon Society and fairly new to the bourbon industry. Kelly Ramsey would soon become a dear friend. Kelly, along with her husband, Forest, is the founder and creator of Art Eatables, Kentucky's premier bourbon chocolatier. Bourbon and chocolate—need I say more? They produce an astonishing array of bourbon-infused chocolate truffles. Each one pairs a popular bourbon with a chocolate specially selected to complement it in an explosion of rich flavor and depth. Kelly and Forest like to say, "These are not your grandma's bourbon balls." The delightful chocolates have enticed many men and women to take their first foray into bourbon country. Kelly has guided me personally through the subtleties of different types of bourbon and how they can be influenced and enhanced by other flavors.

That evening, I tasted, sampled, and listened, and I discovered a new passion. Now I wanted to understand more about this fascinating spirit that has brought together Kentucky's finest for decades and sparked interest in people from all over the world. In fact, in 2007, as part of the declaration to make September National Bourbon Heritage month, bourbon was named "America's Native Spirit" by Congress.

From Bourbon Novice to Bourbon Chocolatier

As a child, Kelly dreamed of a lot of things, but being a bourbon chocolatier was not one of them. In fact, growing up in a Pentecostal home meant alcohol was not even allowed in the house. It wasn't until years later, after she was married, that Kelly had her first taste of bourbon when her husband introduced her to Maker's Mark with a splash of water or Sprite. A foodie and an accomplished home chef, Kelly always loved to explore flavors. She was an avid baker and an amateur candy maker who had started out making confections for holidays and her son's birthday parties. Her friend Lana, who worked for Jim Beam, encouraged Kelly to try other bourbons and discover their complex flavors and nuances. Kelly took up the challenge and thus began her journey.

This was in 2010, when the bourbon boom was just beginning. Lana told Kelly that bourbon companies like Jim Beam were looking for ways to connect with people in different demographics. They were experimenting with ideas to open up the conversation and ease people into the pleasures of bourbon. Kelly and Lana came up with an idea of their own: make candies that taste like cocktails and use them to introduce people to bourbon.

The experimentation commenced. Lana provided Kelly with a list of the bourbon-inspired cocktails, and like a mad scientist Kelly began to play around with flavors and different types of confections. Some combinations were successful, and a few were really bad. The parents of the other kids in her son's soccer league anxiously awaited the samples Kelly brought to weekly games. At first she stuck with all Beam products, experimenting with the flavored whiskies like Red Stag and Jim Beam Honey. The true "aha moment" hit when she began to play with the flagship product on its own, Jim Beam White Label.

Kelly began by first tasting the bourbon. She tried to pick out the different flavor profiles. She tuned in to her senses. She paid attention to the aroma and the taste, where it hit her on the palate, quietly picking out the flavors that lingered. Her first instinct was to combine the bourbon with a dark chocolate, but what she discovered surprised her: the darker chocolate made the flavors off-putting and hot. The next step was to try a wider range of chocolates. For Jim Beam White Label, it turned out, milk chocolate brought out the caramel, vanilla, and wood notes. The bourbon began to taste the way you expected bourbon to taste, without the burn. The right chocolate brought out the bourbon's finest elements.

The big affirming moment came at a party she hosted for the parents of her son's preschool friends. Kelly shared her newest creation with the crowd but did not say what bourbon she had used. One of the guests came up and asked if she had used Jim Beam White Label. It was his favorite bourbon, and he could taste in the chocolate the distinct elements that he already loved so much. Kelly had achieved what she and Lana had set out to do: created a food product that captured and highlighted the taste of Jim Beam bourbon. Once she shared her culinary invention with the folks at Jim Beam, they became her first corporate customer.

Kelly's hobby was quickly becoming a full-time job. She began to work with other major brands like Maker's Mark, Four Roses, and Woodford Reserve. Her mission remained the same: to create an experience with bourbon that was outside the bottle but did not change what was in the bottle. She knew her chocolates were a way for people to taste the best flavors of the bourbon without the intimidation of a straight shot of whiskey. Today she has over 125 different variations of bourbon truffles. Each flavor profile is carefully matched to a specific chocolate. It can range from white chocolate to a milk chocolate with 30 percent cocoa to a dark chocolate with 86 percent cocoa. Each chocolate base is a proprietary blend unique to the specific bourbon.

While Kelly keeps her recipes and trade secrets under lock and key, she did share some of her advice for doing chocolate and bourbon pairing at home. She recommends starting with two bourbons that have different flavor profiles, such as Woodford Reserve and Maker's Mark, and a range of chocolates.

Bourbon and Chocolate Tasting

Recommended Supplies:

Woodford Reserve
Bourbon Whiskey

Maker's Mark Bourbon Whisky

Ghirardelli White
Chocolate Chips

Hershey's Milk Chocolate Bar

Intense Dark Chocolate 86%
Cacao Midnight Reverie Bar

Lindt Excellence Intense
Orange Dark Chocolate Bar

Begin by tasting each bourbon separately, noting what you observe about each one. What aromas do you pick up on? Where do you taste and feel the bourbon on your palate? How does it finish? Do you feel it in your throat or chest? Make note of the differences. (For more in-depth flavor profiles, see bourbon recommendations on pages 12–17.)

Cleanse your palate with a sip of water and/or a plain cracker. Select one of the bourbons and give it a taste, experiencing its full flavor. Take a bit of the white chocolate and savor it for a second. Take a sip of the bourbon and see how the flavors change. Take another bite of the chocolate, this time letting it melt in your mouth and coat your entire tongue. Take one more sip of bourbon and see what you experience.

The chocolate can change the texture of the bourbon and turn it into pure silk. It can also turn a sweet bourbon spicy or bitter. The chocolate will bring out flavors you never knew were there, which can be both good and bad. Keep sampling until you find what you like, and remember, just as with picking your favorite bourbon, there is no right or wrong answer.

So what is bourbon? The first thing you have to remember is that all bourbon is whiskey, but not all whiskey is bourbon. To be called "bourbon," a whiskey must be made in America, consist of at least 51 percent corn, be distilled to 160 proof or less, be put into a barrel at 125 proof or less, and be aged in a new oak vessel, and it cannot contain any additives or flavorings. Don't worry: you don't have to remember all that.

Before I get too technical, let's start by explaining how "whiskey" is made. By definition, whiskey is a spirit distilled from fermented mashed grain. Various grains are used for different varieties of whiskey, including wheat, rye, barley, and corn. Today you will even find exotic grains like quinoa, buckwheat, and oats. The process begins with soaking the grains in warm water and then adding yeast. The yeast breaks down the grain and begins to make sugars, which eventually turn into alcohol. This results in "wort," a soupy substance that gets heated and distilled, separating the solids from the vapors. The vapors become the spirit. The distillate is then aged in wooden barrels.

Whiskey is made all over the world, and different regions produce different types and styles of whiskey, including Scotch, Irish, and American whiskey. Bourbon is the most popular form of American whiskey.

To better understand the process of making bourbon, I met with different distillers at varying stages in their careers and with their own opinions about the process. They all agreed, however, that making bourbon is as much an art as a science.

One of the most recognized names in bourbon is that of master distiller Jim Rutledge. Jim has been in the spirit business since 1966. He began his career at Seagram's and is best known as the master distiller who resurrected the Four Roses brand and raised it to its current glory. Four Roses is a great example of how each component in the process of making bourbon can influence the final outcome. From my first meeting with him, Jim impressed on me that to make a good product, the utmost attention must be paid at every stage of the process, from the selection and inspection of the grain, to the chemical makeup of the water, to the cleanliness of the fermenter. If one element or stage is not right, the final product will not be right.

Whisky vs. Whiskey

Ever since I started the Whisky Chicks, it has been pointed out to me that I am spelling the word "whisky" wrong and that it should be spelled "whiskey." In actuality both spellings are correct, and if you look closely at the labels you will see that famous bourbon brands such as Maker's Mark, George Dickel, and Old Forester spell it "whisky."

According to Wikipedia, the word "whisky" comes from the Gaelic word *uisce* or *uisge*, meaning "water." Many refer to distilled spirits as "aqua vitae" or "water of life." As the word evolved, it was spelled both ways, the way you see different spellings for words like "check" and "cheque" depending on where you are. Upon doing further research, I learned that there are many different opinions on which spelling is right and which one should be used when. For the most part, "whiskey" is used when referring to whiskies made in the United States and Ireland. The spelling "whisky" is generally used in Canada, Japan, Scotland, England, and Wales. One thing was clear, however: always use "whisky" when referring to Scotch. Apparently they take it pretty seriously.

Is Kentucky bourbon whiskey or whisky? Maker's Mark uses "whisky" instead of "whiskey" as part of the Samuels family's tribute to its Scottish heritage. One thing is clear: all bourbon is whiskey but not all whiskey is bourbon, regardless of spelling.

So why Whisky Chicks and not Whiskey Chicks? There are two very simple reasons. The first is that we really liked how "Whisky" had KY at the end, which highlights Kentucky's importance to the world market. The second, and more important, reason is that we did not want to limit the conversation to just Kentucky bourbon or American-style whiskey. Just to be clear: my first and favorite spirit choice will always be some form of Kentucky bourbon, but I have learned that there are many different types of spirits labeled "whisky" from every part of the world, so why limit yourself? It is part of the mission of the Whisky Chicks to not only make Kentucky bourbon the women's drink of choice but to encourage women to take their place along with men in enjoying the many fine spirits this world has to offer.

The Mash Bill

Just like baking bread, what you put into the recipe and how you cook it will determine the flavor. It begins with the mix of grains. Each grain has its own flavor profile. Some are sweet, some are spicy, and some are nutty. Because bourbon always begins with 51 percent or more corn, it is going to have a natural sweetness. The corn is then combined with other grains to create each unique blend. This is called the "mash bill." When you begin trying bourbons, it is best to select those with different types of mash bills because everyone's taste preference is different. Some like the sweetness of a high-wheat bourbon such as Maker's Mark, Larceny, and the infamous Pappy Van Winkle. Others prefer the spiciness that comes with a high-rye bourbon like Four Roses, Bulleit, or Basil Hayden's.

When the grains arrive at the distillery, they go through a series of tests to validate the quality. Some are very scientific and some rely solely on the senses. The simplicity of feeling and smelling the ingredients is reminiscent of the steps any good chef takes when cooking, like smelling the milk or checking the bottle's expiration date to make sure it is fresh. The slightest bit of moisture can cause grains to become musty, and that smell can transfer into the final product. If even the smallest sample of corn from a truck is musty, the entire truck will be rejected. It takes a good nose, commitment, and sometimes a financial investment to remain steadfast.

According to Jim Rutledge, 1997 was a great example of how dedicated Four Roses is to creating a quality product on the front end. That year, Kentucky had an incredibly wet spring. The farmers couldn't even get their crops in the ground until the first of June. This was followed by an extended drought. Corn that would normally grow twelve to fourteen feet was only coming in at seven to eight feet. The cobs and the kernels were much smaller than normal. As part of the quality inspection process, Four Roses would rate the grains on a scale of 1 to 4, with 4 being the highest quality and 1 being an automatic rejection. For months, corn had been coming in steadily at a 4 with no signs of trouble. Jim was out of the country when he received a phone call from his vice president for quality, who said he tested a full truck of corn and it had come in at a 1. They tested another truck with the same results. It appeared that there was a problem with the current crop of corn. Because corn is the primary ingredient for making bourbon, this was a matter of grave concern to the experienced master distiller. Jim immediately returned to the distillery.

How Bourbon is Made

Stage 1
PREPARATION

Whole grains, including corn, wheat, or rye, are dried and ground. Barley goes through a germination process called "malting" where the grain is dampened with water, spread out and allowed to sprout, and then dried, toasted, and ground.

Stage 2
MASHING

In a large cooker or mashtub, the grains are combined with water and cooked to create a liquid known as mash. The enzymes from the malted barley begin to convert the cooked starches into sugar.

Stage 3
FERMENTATION

The mash is cooled and then put in fermenter tanks. Yeast is added, which will convert sugars into alcohol. When it releases the carbon dioxide, it looks like the mixture is boiling. The mixture is about 10 percent alcohol and is referred to as distiller's beer.

Stage 4
DISTILLATION

The fermented liquid is run through a still where it is heated again, converting the alcohol to vapors. The vapors are separated from the liquid and captured. The process is repeated creating a "high wine" or "new make."

Stage 5
MATURATION

Water is added to the new make to bring the barrel entry proof down to at least 125 proof. The distillate will go into new charred oak barrels to age. Once the alcohol hits the barrel, it is technically bourbon. Aging will vary, but a minimum of three to four years is recommended for bourbon.

Stage 6
BOTTLING

The finished product may go directly in the bottle at "cask strength" or be diluted to bring the proof level down. Several barrels may be combined to create a "small batch" bourbon. A "single barrel" will contain liquid from only one barrel.

It was confirmed that the corn was not up to par, and there were concerns that the previous batches that had been processed a few days earlier might have been affected. The decision was made to shut down the entire distillery, clean everything from top to bottom, and begin working on a solution for the corn itself. In classic collaborative form, the first phone calls Jim made were to his competitors, letting them know about the bad corn and alerting them to be on the lookout for it in their distilleries. The Four Roses distillery was shut down for a month. Working together, the distillers found a solution; they aerated the corn, and eventually all returned to normal. The precautions, while expensive, ensured that quality would prevail.

Until I talked with Jim, I had assumed that just as the intense flavors of rye make bourbon spicy, the sweet flavors of wheat make bourbon sweet. Jim explained that the wheat in the mash bill provides little or no flavor. That allows the sugar in the wood to come through and lets each grain impart flavor or complement other components of the distillation process.

For example, Four Roses uses two different mash bills for its bourbon.

75% corn—20% rye—5% malted barley (E)
60% corn—35% rye—5% malted barley (B)

You will note that there is no wheat in these two mash bills. That is because Jim prefers a spicier bourbon with a smooth finish.

The Water

The next key ingredient in making bourbon is the water, and there is nothing better than Kentucky limestone water for making bourbon. Many in the industry would say that the water they are able to source locally is a key differentiator for Kentucky bourbon. The naturally high-calcium water is the perfect complement to other key ingredients, especially the yeast, giving it the nutrients needed to activate the other components in the recipe. Just like the corn, the quality and the chemical makeup will influence the final outcome. Some distillers, like Maker's Mark, will use water from a local limestone spring. Others will use water straight from the tap as long as it comes through the Louisville Water Company, which has been recognized time and time again for the highest-quality, best-tasting tap water in the nation. The key is having high calcium and lower amounts of minerals such as iron, which can ruin the flavor. Some distilleries may put the water through a charcoal filtration to remove impurities, but they always want the calcium to remain on the front end.

Water is used again on the back end to cut down the proof of the final distillate and the aged spirit. That water is usually sent through "reverse osmosis," a process that removes all impurities, including the calcium. Distillers want nothing in the water to affect the flavor or chemical makeup of their final product.

The Yeast

The type of yeast used to cook the grain will also influence flavor. Each distillery has its own yeast strains, many of which were preserved through Prohibition times. The yeast strains are so important to the flavor of the bourbon that some companies have filed patents for their isolated yeasts. The yeast is what influences how the grains cook.

A simple way to think about it is by comparing it once again to baking bread. Yeast from a quick-rise packet is going to produce a bread that tastes very different from bread using a sourdough yeast strain that has been passed on from generation to generation. If you have ever spent time in San Francisco and tasted different sourdough breads, you have detected flavor differences. These come from the different types of yeast used. For years the folks at Seagram's researched various yeast strains, testing and sampling the impact they had on different grains. Jim Rutledge was one of the key researchers on

Photos courtesy of the Kentucky Distiller's Association

Maker's Mark® *Private Select*™

Maker's Mark is one of the world's most recognized top-selling brands of bourbon. They take such immense pride in producing a consistent product that when approached to start a single barrel program, the answer was always no. It did not match who they were. The appeal of a single barrel program is that you are able to choose something unique and different, something that is limited and exclusive, that matches your flavor preferences. How can you do that when the product you produce is all the same?

Jane Thomas Bowie, head of innovation at Maker's Mark, told me that during a conversation she had with owner Bill Samuels Jr. and his son Rob Samuels, Bill shared that in his fifty years in the business the thing he loved and enjoyed the most was making Maker's 46. He was able to take a brand that he knew and loved and make subtle changes to match his palate. Maker's 46 was created by taking ten specially selected one-inch-thick toasted French oak staves and inserting them into a barrel that originally housed Maker's Mark. The barrel was then refilled with mature Maker's Mark, which was aged an additional nine weeks. This simple process amplified the baking spices, especially the cinnamon and vanilla flavors that are already present in Maker's Mark—the flavors that Bill Samuels Jr. enjoys the most.

A light bulb went on. What if Maker's Mark could create a way to develop and enhance the flavors in Maker's Mark to match individual taste preferences? The team worked to find an answer. Together with the Independent Stave Company, they narrowed down the options to five different finishing staves, similar to those used with Maker's 46, that would amplify the flavors in Maker's Mark. Each stave is treated differently to pull out the different flavors.

Maker's Private Select begins with fully matured Maker's Mark at cask strength. Different expressions are created by adding ten custom finishing staves to each barrel and finishing them in their limestone cellar to extract more flavor. The ten finishing staves can be any combination of five flavor profiles chosen especially for this program. With 1,001 possible stave combinations, each expression of Private Select has a customized finish and taste profile that is unique, yet undeniably Maker's.

that team, so it's no surprise that Four Roses uses different yeast strains to produce different flavor profiles.

Just like their mash bills, they classify their different yeast strains and have determined which will produce what type of result based on their chemical makeup.

V: Light fruitiness, light vanilla, caramel, creamy
K: Light spiciness, light caramel, full-bodied
O: Rich fruitiness, light vanilla, caramel, full-bodied
Q: Essence of floral aromas
F: Essence of herbal aromas

The Barrel

When the distillate comes off the still, it is clear and only contains the flavor of the grains. To get that true bourbon flavor and in order for it to be called bourbon, the finished spirit is then placed in a new oak container or barrel. Before the barrels are used, the insides are burnt in a process called "charring." The charring opens up the wood and makes it easier for the wood to impart flavor—but not in the way you might think. Different distilleries use different char levels. The char levels are not just about imparting more or less smoky flavor; they are also about changing the reaction between the wood and the spirit and releasing the sugars into the whiskey.

A good analogy is to think about the different ways to caramelize food, onions being my favorite. When cooked at higher temperatures the sugar within will begin to turn brown and release a delicious sweet, nutty flavor. This same thing occurs within the wood, and depending on on how long it cooks, the flavors and sugars can become more intense. Without getting too technical, it is the wood that plays a big part in those notes of vanilla, brown sugar, caramel, or toffee you taste in bourbon. Char levels are measured by how long the barrel's interior is exposed to intense heat:

Level 1 char—15 seconds
Level 2 char—30 seconds
Level 3 char—35 seconds
Level 4 char—55 seconds

Level 4 char is also known as the "alligator char" because it creates a texture similar to alligator hide.

The size of the barrel also affects the flavors and the aging process. The standard size barrel that you see in most distilleries holds fifty-three gallons. To accelerate the aging process there are several distilleries that experiment with different size barrels ranging from three gallons to thirty gallons. It is all about the surface area. Smaller barrels have a higher ratio of surface area to spirit, which allows the whiskey to capture the flavors from the wood much faster.

The Aging Process

There are no aging requirements for a whiskey to be called a bourbon. But to be called a "straight bourbon," it has to be aged for at least two years in the barrel. There are bourbons on the market that have been aged as little as three months and others that have been aged more than twenty years. The longer a spirit sits in the barrel, the more flavors will be imparted into the whiskey. According to most bourbon aficionados, there is not an ideal age for bourbon, though many prefer bourbons aged between eight and twelve years. Most in the industry will agree that it generally takes four years for a bourbon to achieve the right flavor balance. As part of the aging process, weather and storage conditions also play a role in the development of a bourbon's flavors. Even then you can have two barrels made with the same ingredients, coming from the same batch of distillate in the same barrels, aged in the same part of the warehouse, that taste completely different.

Who knew all this science and work went into making bourbon!

For the Love of Bourbon

THREE | *For the Love of Bourbon*

I have to tell you how bourbon may have saved my career. The first time I went to a fine restaurant with a business client, I felt so intimidated. I was barely twenty-one, and while I had been out to nice places to eat before, I had never had to worry about what to drink or how to order. I was afraid I would do something stupid. My boss was a very large, imposing man, probably six foot six and over three hundred pounds. He had moved to Kentucky from New York, and it was abundantly clear he was much more sophisticated than I was. I was invited to join him for dinner with a very important customer, with whom I had formed a bond and who had specifically asked that I attend.

While I was flattered, I was incredibly nervous. We were seated, menus were presented, and the wine list was left on the table. Up until this point I had never seen anyone order from a wine list. My dad would always ask for a glass of ice with his white wine if that gives you any clue about my wine experience. Our waiter asked about what type of wine we liked, and I confidently said white zinfandel, which was greeted with slight chuckles from my dinner companions. Of course they ordered something much nicer. I am not sure what it was other than it was red and it didn't taste anything like the Cella Lambrusco my parents used to drink. During this one dinner I was introduced to so many new things. I think we ordered calamari for an appetizer, which I later learned was squid; an entree with duck confit (which I confused with confetti and was not sure what to expect); and a fabulously rich dessert that was lit on fire tableside at the end of the evening. We were then asked if we wanted an after-dinner cocktail. My boss ordered some type of brandy, and our client ordered a glass of port. I ordered what my favorite aunt would have ordered, a Maker's Mark on the rocks. That won this inexperienced twenty-one-year-old some immediate respect.

I cannot tell you how many times over the years I have heard "There is something about a woman drinking bourbon." Why yes, there is! We know what we want, and we are not afraid to ask for it. But many women are not sure what to ask for. Do they order it neat, straight up, on the rocks, with a twist, shaken, or stirred? Some just scratch their heads, declare they are too confused, and ask for beer or a glass of wine. I am here to tell you, there is only one right way to drink bourbon and that is the way *you* like it.

Whisky Chicks, Amber & Maggie, taking part in a bourbon tasting. *Photo courtesy of Leah Pottinger.*

I always recommend that if you are just starting your bourbon journey, take it slow, experiment with different cocktails, then work your way to "on the rocks" or "neat." If you are a wine drinker, chances are you did not start out drinking a heavy cabernet or zinfandel. You probably began with a white zinfandel, a chianti, or even something sweeter. It took time tasting and experiencing different types of wine before you discovered your absolute favorites and what brands and blends you prefer. I have been honored to walk alongside many women as they began their bourbon journey. Each began with a natural curiosity and interest in learning about the famed brown spirit. Each journey, like each person, is unique, and it begins one step at a time. For many, that first sip can be the hardest, but it doesn't have to be, especially when you have confidence in what you are ordering.

Just like wines, your favorite bourbon brands can come in different styles and expressions (different versions of the same whiskey), each with its own flavors and profile. Certain terms are used to explain the differences and help you anticipate what's inside the bottle. Most of the information you need to know is on the bottle itself. As referenced earlier, to be called bourbon, the spirit must be made in the United States from at least 51 percent corn, distilled no higher than 160 proof, put into a barrel at no higher than 125 proof, and put in a new charred oak container. To be called "Kentucky bourbon," the bourbon must be produced and then aged for a minimum of one year in the state of Kentucky. To be called a "straight bourbon," it must be aged a minimum of two years.

In the last few years, many top producers have come out with "single barrel" and "small batch" versions of their products. Although Old Forester was one of the first to market a single barrel in the 1950s, Blanton's was one of the first to mass-market a single barrel bourbon. There is no legal definition for "single barrel," but as the name implies, all of the bourbon in the bottle does come from a single barrel. Many times, single barrel bourbons will be undiluted and will be a higher proof. The higher the proof, the higher the percentage of alcohol and the stronger the spirit will usually be.

The term "small batch" also has no legal definition. Different distilleries follow different guidelines for what they label small batch bourbon. For instance, Elijah Craig selects a limited number of barrels that best match the flavor profile Heaven Hill has for the brand. They then marry them together to ensure consistency. The key phrase is "limited number of barrels." There is no standard amount that determines the title "small batch"; for Elijah Craig twelve-year-old small batch, fewer than eighty barrels are mixed together.

Another common term used for classifying bourbon is "bottled in bond." Back in the nineteenth century, almost any brown spirit could be called bourbon. It was an unregulated industry with an ongoing battle between whiskey distillers and whiskey rectifiers. Rectifiers would obtain their whiskey from a variety of sources, adding color and flavor to produce bourbon knockoffs. When buying a bottle of bourbon, one could not be sure of the quality or even the safety of the product. Colonel E. H. Taylor Jr., who was known for making high-quality bourbon, fought hard to develop and enforce regulations that would ensure consistency in the bourbon industry. This is when the 1897 Bottled-in-Bond Act came into existence, ensuring that any whiskey bearing the label "bottled in bond" was produced by the same distiller at the same distillery during the same distilling season, aged for at least four years, unadulterated (save for pure water for dilution), and bottled at exactly 100 proof. The label also had to identify the distillery where the whiskey was distilled and bottled.

How to Read a Bourbon Label

Age Statement
for Kentucky Bourbon
is required if less than
four years.

Brand Name
cannot imply an age
or country of origin that
is untrue.

Name and Location
identify where the product was made
and bottled (these stages may not
have occurred at the same place).

AGED IN NEW OAK BARRELS
A MINIMUM OF 4 YEARS

This is the place
where your brand
story goes. Tell
people about what
makes your spirit
special, but keep it
true and honest.
Consumers want
authenticity when
buying spirits.

HANDCRAFTED PRODUCT

BADASS BOURBON

KENTUCKY STRAIGHT BOURBON WHISKY

DISTILLED AND BOTTLED BY
BADASS DISTILLING CO.

46.5% ALC/VOL (93 PROOF)

**Distilled and Bottled by
Badass Distilling Co.,
123 Main Street
Louisville, Kentucky**

GOVERNMENT WARNING:
(1) According to the Surgeon
General, women should not
drink alcoholic beverages
during pregnancy because of
the risk of birth defects.
(2) Consumption of alcoholic
beverages impairs your ability
to drive a car or operate
machinery, and may cause
health problems.

750 ML

Net Contents
must be stated
in metric units.

Class or Type
must meet the specific
requirements for
different classifications.

Alcohol by Volume
must legally be
stated as a %
of volume.

A Government Warning
is required on all products
with 0.5% alcohol by
volume or higher.

90 PROOF

100 PROOF

FIRST BOTTLED BOURBON

FIRST BOTTLED BOURBON

ESTD 1870 OLD FORESTER 1870
KENTUCKY STRAIGHT BOURBON WHISKY

In 1870, George Garvin Brown crafted the original small batch whiskey at 311 West Main Street on Louisville's Whiskey Row. The Old Forester 1870 expression is hand-crafted in this tradition.

750mL 45% ALCOHOL BY VOLUME (90 PROOF)

ESTD 1870 OLD FORESTER 1897
KENTUCKY STRAIGHT BOURBON WHISKY

With the passage of the Bottled in Bond Act of 1897, Old Forester transitioned from 90 proof to 100 proof. Originally produced on Louisville's Whiskey Row, this whiskey has a rich, bold character reminiscent of a 19th-century bourbon.

750mL 50% ALCOHOL BY VOLUME (100 PROOF)

Photo courtesy of Brown Forman

The Story of Old Forester

Old Forester began in 1870 when George Garvin Brown, a pharmaceutical salesman, saw an opportunity in the market. At the time, whiskey was a popular medication for relieving a number of ailments. In his experience with physicians, he observed that the common complaints about medicinal whiskey were inconsistency and poor quality. For the most part, the whiskey industry was unregulated at this time. Whiskey was purchased by the barrel, which allowed multiple opportunities to compromise the final product before it reached the end consumer. Stretching product to maximize profits was common practice and was achieved by adding such items as tobacco juice, iodine, and paint thinner. Because a barrel is an opaque vessel whose contents can be tampered with, the whiskey on the market was far from ideal.

George had a plan to offer a product that would be consistent, packaged in a nonreactive container, and of a quality that he and physicians would be proud to stand behind. Old Forester was born, the first bourbon to be sold exclusively in sealed glass bottles. The brand was a game changer for the entire industry and is the founding brand of the Brown-Forman company. It has never been off the market since its conception, but market trends have taken its success on a roller coaster ride. The brand was based on a philosophy of doing what is right, with quality, family, and ingenuity at the forefront. These same principles are driving the brand forward in a competitive market cluttered with gimmicks, restoring it to its rightful place. As George advertised, there is nothing better on the market.

Many brands have risen, failed, and been bought or traded in this industry. Old Forester is the only brand owned and produced by the same company before, during, and after Prohibition. Two factors enabled this. The first is that Brown-Forman held KY Permit No. 3, which under the parameters of the 18th Amendment and the authority of the Treasury Department allowed the company to sell Old Forester as medicinal whiskey throughout Prohibition. That permit let the brand remain present through the thirteen-year dry spell. The second is the Brown family's commitment to the continuation of the brand George Garvin Brown created.

Special thanks to the team at Old Forester for providing the history and heritage of one of the country's oldest and most recognized brands of bourbon.

Others will classify bourbons by their mash bill or their recipe of grains. Legend has it that Marge Samuels, wife of Maker's Mark founder Bill Samuels, made 150 different loaves of bread to select the original Maker's Mark mash bill. It was the sweetness and the softness of the wheat bread that appealed to the elder Samuels, and this is how they came up with the recipe they follow today. Maker's Mark is often referred to as a wheated bourbon. Other popular wheated bourbons include Larceny, W. L. Weller, and my personal favorite, 1792 Sweet Wheat (limited release). High-rye bourbons generally have 20 percent or more rye as part of their mash bill. Just like rye bread, high ryes will have a bit more spice to them. While this is not always true, I have found that high-rye bourbons start off spicy but finish smoother. Popular high-rye bourbons include Basil Hayden's, Bulleit, Old Forester, and Woodford Reserve. To determine which flavors you prefer, choose one to two from each category and do a side-by-side tasting. That is the only way to determine what you like.

A tasting flight for someone just starting out might look like this: **Basil Hayden's (80 proof high rye)**, **Bulliet (90 proof high rye)**, **Makers Mark (wheated 90 proof)**, and **1792 (wheated 93.7 proof)**.

This lineup allows you to compare different mash bills, but it also shows a gradual increase in proof. Each of these bourbons is produced by a different distillery and is easy to find at most liquor stores across the United States.

So how do you do a bourbon tasting? Start with selecting the bourbon. A tasting can be as simple as comparing two different bourbons, or you can create a flight of bourbon by selecting three or more different bourbons. Flights are a great way to compare and contrast different bourbons. When choosing your bourbons, there is no right or wrong answer. Depending on where you live, your tasting may be based on what you can find in your local liquor store. Tastings can be about comparing or highlighting style, age, proof, producers, regions, mash bills, and so on.

To prepare for your tasting, I recommend you begin with the setups. I always begin with paper and pen for taking notes, small bites of select ingredients, a glass of water, a straw, a cup of ice, and a bottle of my favorite ginger ale. You won't find ginger ale at most tastings. The Whisky Chicks make it available because we understand that many of our guests are at different places in their journey, and they need the added sweetness of the ginger ale to soften the taste of the bourbon. Once they have acquired and

appreciate the different flavors of bourbon, they will begin to wean themselves off the ginger ale, moving to water, ice, and then drinking it straight.

There is much debate over what type of glass to use for a tasting. The most recommended tasting glass is the Glencairn whiskey glass. Its tulip shape that narrows at the top is designed to capture the nose of the spirit. For beginners, any glass will do, but we do recommend that all the tastings be done in the same type of glass. Even though it may be frowned upon by some, for convenience and consistency you can purchase small clear plastic shot glasses from your local liquor or party supply store. In each glass, pour about a half ounce of bourbon.

Tasting bourbon truly engages all the senses. Begin by looking at the liquid in the glass. What color do you see? Generally, the darker the color, the longer it has been aged. Swirl it around in the glass a bit. Just like wine, bourbon will have "legs" that drip down the inside of the glass. The thinner the legs, the higher the proof. Bourbons also have different viscosity. Some may be thick, oily, or water-like.

The next step is "nosing" the bourbon. Begin by swirling the liquid around to incorporate air and release some of the alcohol. This will help release more of the aromas. With your mouth open, take a sniff. Be careful not to stick your nose straight into the glass. The alcohol vapors from a high-proof bourbon can numb your nose. Take it slow and gently inhale the aromas

MICHAEL VEACH, a renowned bourbon historian, likes to recommend that you take a walk through a village, as he describes in an October 2013 article in the *Lexington Herald-Leader*:

"The wood shop": oak, pecan, hazelnut, or cedar

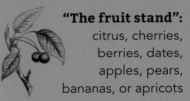

"The fruit stand": citrus, cherries, berries, dates, apples, pears, bananas, or apricots

"The candy shop": vanilla, caramel, cloves, anise, or licorice

"The spice shop": cinnamon, nutmeg, or pepper

"The floral shop": rose, honeysuckle, or lilac

of the bourbon. Place the glass down for a few seconds, take a deep breath in and out to clear your senses, and then take a second sniff. What do you smell? Grasses, nuts, fruits, spices, herbs? Take time to focus and concentrate, and write down your first reaction. Sometimes we smell things but do not have the language to describe it. That is where a flavor wheel can come in handy. When nosing a bourbon, there is no right or wrong answer. You smell what you smell, but I have learned that the power of suggestion can influence your perception.

The next step is actually tasting the bourbon. This is a good point to remind your guests that they should be sipping the bourbon and not shooting it like a Jäger bomb. They are going to come back and experiment with the different bourbons so they should conserve the samples you have provided. To truly capture all of the flavors of bourbon, you want to take a small sip and roll it around in your mouth. This was aptly named the "Kentucky Chew" by Fred Noe, master distiller of Jim Beam. Let it coat your tongue, taking note of where you feel and taste it the most. Is it on the back of your tongue, the sides, or right in the middle? How does it feel when you swallow it? Does it have a smooth finish or does it burn going down? How long does the burn last? Note how the bourbon feels in your mouth: is it oily, thick, or just plain hot? If you can feel it in your throat and your chest, that is called the "Kentucky Hug."

After taking your first sip, pause a moment and then take a second sip. Does anything change? Note the differences. Referring back to your flavor wheel, write down the flavors you taste. It is important to note that not everyone will taste the same thing. Some palates will pick up on flavors that even the master distiller never catches, and some can only distinguish what they like and don't like. One story I have heard many times is about a master distiller who was asked by an audience member how he got the cherry and vanilla notes in his bourbon to pop. The distiller paused for a moment and said, "Well, I don't know about all of those things that people always pick out of our bourbon. I just know good bourbon and bad bourbon." He then took a sip of his bourbon and declared, "That there, that's a good bourbon!" Sometimes that is all you need to get from a tasting: a clear idea of what you like and don't like.

For some palates, a straight taste of bourbon is too much. That is when we introduce other elements into the tasting. The first thing we recommend is that you begin by using your straw to add a single drop of water or a piece of ice. It is amazing what that will do to open the bourbon and allow the flavors to come through. In most cases it will

Flavor Wheel

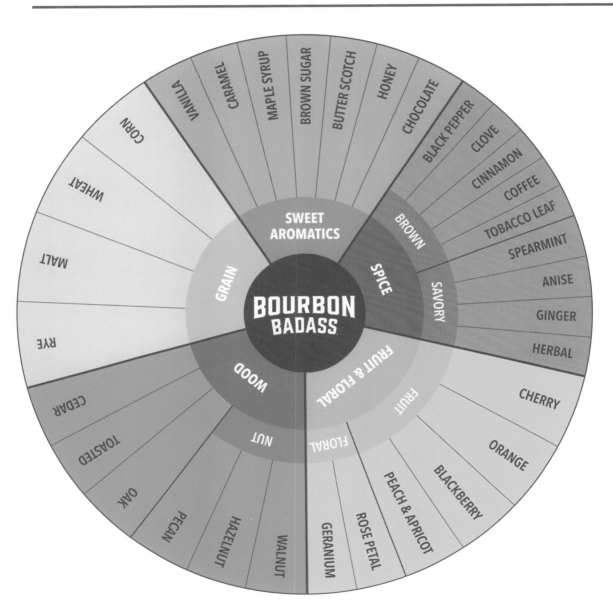

soften the bourbon and smooth out the rough edges of the finish. Note the differences in flavors. Refer back to your flavor wheel to see if you are able to discern flavors much better than before.

To highlight the differences in the bourbon, experiment with accompanying flavors and textures. If the bourbon is still too strong, you can add a few drops of ginger ale. This will increase the sweetness but still allow the flavors of the bourbon to come through. I always like to have a few small bites available to demonstrate how food can influence the palate and bring out certain flavors and depress others. We have paired bourbon with chocolates, nuts, olives, dried fruits, cheeses, and smoked meats, but nothing is off-limits. Move around the different bourbons in your lineup. Tasting different bourbons back to back can reveal aspects of the spirit that you didn't previously notice. Take notes along the way.

After you have had a chance to sample and taste and figure out what you like or don't like, look for similarities in your choices. Are they close to the same proof or age? Are they all single barrels or small batch? Do they seem to come from one single producer? Do they have a similar mash bill? Are they all bottled in bond? Now that you know what all of this means, you can confidently walk into any bar and order what you like the way you like it.

How to Order a Bourbon

Once you discover your favorite bourbon and are able to pick out the right one from a list at a restaurant, it helps to understand the different ways you can order your bourbon. Here is a quick glossary of terms to help.

Neat
The straight spirit in a glass without ice or a mixer

On the rocks
The straight spirit served over ice with no mixers

Straight up
Some type of cocktail or spirit that has been chilled with ice but is strained and served without ice, usually in a martini glass

With a twist
A fruit garnish, usually a citrus peel, twisted and rubbed around the rim of the glass and added to the spirit or cocktail

NOTE: When ordering a spirit neat or on the rocks, you might see an extra charge on your bill. The first time it occurred to me I thought they were charging me for the ice and was pretty upset. But it's not about the ice. A standard cocktail generally has 1.5 ounces of liquor, while a spirit on the rocks or neat will be a 2-ounce pour, thus justifying the minimal increase, which is usually $2.

Any Way
You Want It

FOUR | *Any Way You Want It*

The first Whisky Chicks event was held in January 2014 at one of the country's best whiskey bars, Down One Bourbon Bar. The private dining room is reminiscent of a speakeasy from the Prohibition era. Hidden behind the bright red British-style phone booth was the perfect setting for an amazing ladies' night out, featuring fine spirits, delicious appetizers, and new friends. It was less than six degrees outside, and Louisville, for the most part, was shut down due to the unexpected extreme cold. There was concern that no one would show up, other than a few loyal friends who had pledged their support for this new venture. I knew I was onto something when over thirty-five women attended, eager to meet other women who were adventurous and curious about bourbon. That evening we enjoyed a specialty cocktail made just for us and a delectable array of appetizers to complement the evening's festivities.

After our first event, we were inspired. The wheels were in motion to pursue our mission: to introduce more women to the pleasures of whiskey, especially Kentucky bourbon whiskey. Our next event had to be a full-blown bourbon tasting. Haymarket Whiskey Bar has been listed on numerous national and international lists of top bourbon bars, including that of *The Bourbon Review*. The owner agreed to be our host.

Food is always a crucial component of any Whisky Chicks event. To set the mood for the evening, a stunning spread of bourbon-inspired bites was prepared, including a tray of assorted cheeses and charcuterie, like brie with dried apples, cranberries, and bourbon caramel sauce.

Tickets for this event quickly sold out. It was a full house and everyone was thrilled. Our host carefully selected a variety of bourbons, including popular brands

Whisky Chicks Sunrise

Fill a glass with ice, add 2 ounces of Old Forester 86 Proof Bourbon Whisky, 1 ounce simple syrup, and 1 ounce Triple Sec. Stir vigorously. Squeeze and add a small wedge of lemon. Serve.

and relative unknowns. We all gathered together, eager to learn what we could about bourbon. The tables had been set with tasting mats and a sampling of five or six bourbons. He began by sharing his knowledge and passion for the Kentucky-made spirit. He told of the history, the facts, the important details about what makes all bourbon whiskey but not all whiskey bourbon. Not knowing the proper protocol for a tasting, we sat listening intently, trying to take in every word he said. About ten to fifteen minutes into his talk, someone broke the ice and politely asked if it was okay to taste the bourbon samples in front of each of us. Laughing, our host explained that a typical tasting group would have already downed what was in front of them and be asking for more. He realized then that we wanted a guide for our journey. He backtracked and patiently began to introduce us to each sample one by one.

Most of us, including me, had always drunk bourbon either over ice or in some type of cocktail. Drinking bourbon straight was new and a little intimidating. I don't remember what it was that we tasted first, but I do recall it being very strong with a harsh burn. It did not make me want to take a second sip. I wasn't alone in this: as I looked around the room, the silence signaled displeasure and the faces revealed distaste. We moved onto our second bourbon. This was a little better than the first. As I recall there was a slightly smoother finish and what I began to recognize as flavors like vanilla, dark cherry, and a slight hint of caramel along with the

Brie with Dried Apple, Cranberries, Pecans, and Bourbon Caramel Sauce

Ingredients:

¼ cup chopped, dried apples

¼ cup dried cranberries

¼ cup chopped pecans

2 tablespoons bourbon

¼ cup caramel ice cream topping

1 small round of brie

Soak chopped apples, dried cranberries, and chopped pecans with bourbon. Let sit for at least 30 minutes, up to 2 hours, allowing the bourbon to soak into the fruit and nuts. Stir caramel ice cream topping into fruit mixture. Pour onto brie, and serve with your favorite bread. Best served at room temperature.

smokiness of the oak. Many of the others, however, were probably ready to chalk this up as an "interesting" experience that they didn't want to repeat.

Haymarket Whiskey Bar did their best to keep the women in the room engaged, but after the second tasting, the intimidation factor was too much. One brave woman in the back of the room raised her hand above the crowd and asked the best question of the night. It not only helped salvage the evening but also forever transformed the way in which the Whisky Chicks approach events. She asked, "I don't usually drink bourbon. I drink mainly wine. What is the best way for me to learn about and experience bourbon?" For our host, who had been asked this question before, a light went on. He quickly said, "I would start with an Old Fashioned and work my way up." He followed up by asking the room, "How many of you are not regular bourbon drinkers?" All but a few hands in the room went up. Asking the group to be patient, he said he would be right back. A few minutes later he returned with trays of Old Fashioned cocktails for the crowd. With this one quick adaptation, frowns turned to smiles and the tasting event turned into a success.

I am still convinced we scared a few people off that night. There were folks I have not seen since, and that taught me a valuable lesson: if you are going to introduce someone to bourbon or any kind of whiskey for the first time, starting with a straight shot will not yield optimum results. Outside of designated whiskey tastings, at every event since our first one, the Whisky Chicks have gone out of their way to ensure there is something delicious and interesting for everyone, including the novice, the enthusiast, and the connoisseur. Each time, we try to have a different cocktail that is simple to make and introduces different styles of bourbon and whiskey. So if you are a beginner, skip the straight shot and instead combine the bourbon with some of your favorite flavors for a sipping cocktail.

Cocktails have played an important role in the history of bourbon and whiskey. In fact, the Museum of the American Cocktail in New Orleans is dedicated to educating and preserving the history of mixology. The origins of the term "cocktail" have been debated over the years. In 1803, the *Farmer's Cabinet*, an agricultural periodical published in Philadelphia, first used the word "cocktail" to refer to a drink—and not to a horse with a shortened tail. One of the first definitions appeared in the *Balance and Columbian*

Bacon-Wrapped Dates with Bourbon Glaze

At our first event at Down One Bourbon Bar, not only did we enjoy fabulous bourbon cocktails but were also served delicious appetizers, including bacon-wrapped dates with bourbon glaze. After that evening, food has always been a central part of a Whisky Chicks experience.

Ingredients:
½ cup bourbon
¾ cup brown sugar
¾ cup butter
16 pitted Medjool dates
16 teaspoons Gorgonzola cheese
8 slices bacon

Prepare sauce by combining bourbon with brown sugar and butter in a small saucepan. Cook until sugar dissolves and mixture begins to boil slightly. Remove from heat and set aside. Cut dates in half, filling one side of the date with a teaspoon of Gorgonzola cheese. Top with other half and wrap with ½ piece of bacon. Secure with a toothpick. Sear in a large sauté pan over medium high heat. Once bacon begins to brown, top with sauce and place in 325° oven for 10 to 15 minutes.

Repository (Hudson, New York) on May 13, 1806. Editor Harry Croswell answered the question "What is a cocktail?"

Cock-tail is a stimulating liquor, composed of spirits of any kind, sugar, water, and bitters—it is vulgarly called bittered sling, and is supposed to be an excellent electioneering potion, in as much as it renders the heart stout and bold, at the same time that it fuddles the head. It is said also to be of great use to a democratic candidate because a person, having swallowed a glass of it, is ready to swallow anything else.

— Harry Croswell, *Balance and Columbian Repository* (Hudson, New York), 1806.

The first recorded "Cocktail Party" was held in 1917. Mrs. Julius S. Walsh Jr. of St. Louis, Missouri, was reported to have invited fifty friends over to her mansion for a one-hour party of drinking and merriment, which she termed "a Cocktail Party." A variety of drinks were served, including Martinis and Manhattans. This was seen as an innovation, and Mrs. Walsh even received public praise for the idea in the newspapers.

Not surprisingly, our preferred cocktails begin with Kentucky bourbon or rye. We keep it simple by combining our favorite spirits with different types of bitters and simple syrups to create delectable cocktails that are easily mixed and shared with a friend or a big crowd.

Simple Syrup

Sugar and water can be combined in the form of ice and a packet of sugar, or a syrup can be made from boiling sugar and water together. Simple syrups can be infused with different flavors, including herbs (basil, thyme, or rosemary), fruits (apples, oranges, or blackberries), spices (cinnamon, clove, or black pepper), or any combination of these. You are limited only by your imagination. Simple syrups are not only used to create delicious bourbon cocktails but are also great with seltzer water. You can buy simple syrups at specialty food stores and some liquor stores, but they are so easy to make that we encourage you to create your own.

Basic Simple Syrup

Boil together 1 cup sugar and 1 cup water. Refrigerate for up to 4 weeks in an airtight container.

Infused Simple Syrup

Boil together 1 cup sugar and 1 cup water. While hot, add herbs, whole spices, or citrus rind. Cover for an hour and let cool. Remove added ingredients. Can be refrigerated for up to 2 weeks in an airtight container.

Possible infusions include basil, rosemary, black peppercorn, vanilla beans, cinnamon sticks, cloves, nutmeg, ginger, fresh or dried chilies, or various citrus rinds like grapefruit or lime.

Mint Julep Syrup

Boil together 1 cup sugar, 1 cup water, and a large bunch of fresh spearmint. Let sit on stove for 30 minutes until cooled. Remove mint leaves and strain syrup through a coffee filter. Can be refrigerated for up to 2 weeks in an airtight container.

Strawberry Simple Syrup

Boil together 1 cup sugar, 1 cup water, 1 cup chopped strawberries, and 1 tablespoon vanilla. Let sit on stove for 30 minutes until cooled. Strain syrup through a coffee filter. Can be refrigerated for up to 2 weeks in an airtight container.

Blackberry Basil Syrup

Boil together 1 cup sugar, 1 cup water, 1 cup blackberries, and 6–8 large fresh basil leaves. Let sit on stove for 30 minutes until cooled. Remove basil leaves and strain syrup through a coffee filter. Can be refrigerated for up to 2 weeks in an airtight container.

Blackberry Basil Syrup

Jalapeño Apple Syrup

Boil together 1 cup sugar, 1 cup water, 2 large Granny Smith apples (sliced with peel on), and 1 jalapeño pepper (sliced; seeds can be removed to reduce heat). Let sit on stove for 30 minutes until cooled. Remove apple slices and pepper. Strain syrup through a coffee filter; repeat. Can be refrigerated for up to 2 weeks in an airtight container.

Peach Vanilla Bean Simple Syrup

Boil together 1 cup sugar, 1 cup water, 2–3 medium-size peaches (peeled and sliced), and 1 whole vanilla bean, split open. Let sit on stove for 30 minutes until cooled. Remove peaches and vanilla. Strain syrup through a coffee filter; repeat. Can be refrigerated for up to 2 weeks in an airtight container.

Pumpkin Spice Simple Syrup

Boil together 1 cup brown sugar and 1 cup water. After sugar has dissolved, add ¼ cup canned pumpkin, 3 cinnamon sticks, and ½ teaspoon each of ginger, nutmeg, and cloves. Let simmer for 5–10 minutes. Turn off heat and let it cool on the stove. Strain syrup through a coffee filter; repeat. Can be refrigerated for up to 2 weeks in an airtight container.

Bitters

Not until I began to learn about bourbon did I discover what bitters actually are and how they are used to add and enhance the flavor of a cocktail. Traditionally, bitters are an alcoholic solution flavored with botanicals characterized by a bitter, sour, or bitter-sweet flavor. Brands of bitters were originally developed for medicinal purposes, but are now sold as digestifs and cocktail flavorings. The botanical ingredients used in preparing bitters have historically consisted of aromatic herbs, bark, roots, and/or fruit for their flavor and medicinal properties. Most bitters contain both water and alcohol. The alcoholic strength of bitters varies widely across different brands and styles, but you usually only need a dash or two to add flavor. They are like the salt and pepper of the cocktail world.

The range of bitters available has increased dramatically over the years. The most commonly known type and the one on most bar shelves is Angostura®. In 1824, Dr. Johann Siegert first produced these aromatic bitters as a medicinal tincture designed to alleviate stomach ailments. The recipe itself is closely guarded. It is a nice spicy, fresh, orange-flavored bitter that can enhance the flavor of a whiskey and other spirits. Think about the flavors you like in baking and chances are you can find a bitter that brings that flavor to life in your cocktail. One of our favorite collections of bitters comes from Fee Brothers, who refer to their assortment as the "spice rack behind the bar," with flavors like chocolate, cardamom, grapefruit, and rhubarb. Bitters will help round out and balance the flavors of a cocktail, stimulating the bitter receptors on the tongue. In a well-made cocktail, bitters balance out the sweet and the sour. The great thing about bitters is that just a dash or two will add incredible flavor, and if stored properly a small bottle will retain its flavor for three to five years.

The Cherry on Top

The popular bright red maraschino cherry is a staple on most bars. I remember as a kid feeling so grown up when my dad ordered me my very own cocktail, a Shirley Temple with extra cherries. It took having a Manhattan with Luxardo cherries to open me up to a whole new world of cherries. At fifteen dollars a jar, Luxardo cherries are as far as you can get from the average waxy sugary-sweet maraschino cherry you find on top of an ice cream sundae. In doing research, I discovered that Luxardo was a distillery on the Croatian coast that created its very own cherry liqueur, which they called maraschino. In 1905, they began selling the cherries in jars, thus creating the first maraschino cherry. Around Prohibition time, Ernest Wiegand, a horticulturist at Oregon Agricultural College, found a way to create his own version of maraschino cherries by adding almond flavoring and red food dye. They soon became very popular in cocktails, and the original Luxardo maraschino cherry was soon replaced in the market with the version we know today.

After playing around with a few different versions, I came up with a recipe for creating your own Luxardo maraschino cherries at home.

Homemade Luxardo Cherries

Ingredients:

½ cup white sugar
1 tablespoon real vanilla
1 cinnamon stick
A pinch of nutmeg
2 tablespoons lemon juice
½ cup water
1 pound frozen cherries
1 cup Luxardo liqueur

In a medium saucepan combine sugar, vanilla, cinnamon stick, nutmeg, lemon juice, and water. Bring to a boil for 2–3 minutes. Turn the heat down to low. Add cherries and let simmer for about 5 minutes until sauce begins to thicken slightly. Remove from heat and add the liqueur. Let cool, and store in airtight container in refrigerator.

Optional: Replace Luxardo liqueur with ½ cup of your favorite bourbon

Recommended: When all of the cherries are gone, reduce the juice into a sauce and serve over ice cream or a bowl of mixed berries. It is delicious!

Classic Old Fashioned

To appreciate and experience the different layers of a cocktail, I like to guide people through the assembly of a classic Old Fashioned. A mixologist would probably tell you the steps are out of order and a little unorthodox, but that is intentional. The goal is for you to taste and experience how each ingredient influences the final outcome of this classic cocktail, kind of like your own personal bourbon tasting.

What you will need: bourbon, ice, simple syrup, bitters, orange peel

Spirit—Every good cocktail begins with the spirit. For a classic Old Fashioned we like to use a classic bourbon like Old Forester 86. Fill a two-ounce shot glass and take in the aroma of the bourbon. Using the flavor wheel on page 55, try to identify the different fragrances. Take a small sip and note the flavors that come through and where you feel them the most on your palate and in your throat.

Water/Ice—Add either a small piece of ice or a couple drops of water to the bourbon. Swirl it around and give it another smell. Note the change. Just a few drops of water cause the alcohol to dissipate and bring out new flavor notes. Take another small sip and you will see how the flavors of the bourbon are able to shine through.

Simple syrup—Fill a rocks glass with ice and add the bourbon. I don't like really sweet drinks, therefore I start out with a half ounce of simple syrup. You can add more based on your taste preference. Swirl it around and take a small sip. The flavors of the bourbon should still be prominent, but for some, the added sweetness makes it more palatable.

Bitters—For a classic Old Fashioned, we recommend Angostura. Add a dash or two to the cocktail and mix with a spoon or a swirl of the glass. Now take another taste and experience how the flavors really come alive. This cocktail is perfect for experimenting with bitters, including chocolate, cherry, and black walnut. Each one will bring out a different flavor in the bourbon.

Orange peel—Take a piece of orange peel, between one and a half and two inches long, and twist it in the glass, releasing the essential oils. Take the outer peel and run it along the rim of the glass. Now taste the cocktail. This last step is one that I always thought was part of the theater of creating a cocktail, but I soon realized the orange peel adds that finishing touch that brightens the whole cocktail.

The Pappy Phenomenon

When Pappy Van Winkle is released every year, it seems the news is *the* topic of conversation when it comes to bourbon. If you have ever had it, the challenge of getting a new bottle is planted in your head. If you have never had it, you are probably at least curious about why everyone wants to get it. It seems everyone thinks this is the best bourbon out there, with a price to match.

So, what is all the excitement about? The Pappy legend has a long history in Kentucky and can be traced back to when the original Julian Van Winkle, or Pappy, as he was known, started working for W. L. Weller as a salesman. Sally Van Winkle's great book, *But Always a Fine Bourbon*, describes the Van Winkles' contributions to the bourbon industry and the family history in more detail. Early releases of the bourbon came from the Stitzel-Weller distillery. This distillery has a cult following of its own; old bottles distilled there are cherished and collected today. As those old barrels are being used up, new barrels are being made at the Buffalo Trace distillery in Frankfort, Kentucky.

Although all of the Van Winkle brands have been well respected and popular, the world started to really take notice after a couple of key events brought widespread and ongoing media attention to this truly American spirit and its devotees. The first was in 1996, when the twenty-year bourbon was submitted to the Beverage Testing Institute and received an unprecedented 99 rating. The second was when Julian Van Winkle III won the Outstanding Spirits Professional award from the James Beard Foundation in 2011.

There are many components involved in determining the final product. One of the key ingredients of a bourbon recipe is the mash bill—the combination of grains used. Bourbon has to be made from at least 51 percent corn. The remaining grains vary by type and distillery preference. Rye, malted barley, or wheat typically make up the balance, but some new grains are now being introduced, creating new flavor profiles.

The Van Winkle bourbons are made using a wheated mash bill. This gives it a sweeter flavor, and it is generally smoother compared to other common mash bills that use rye as the second grain. While bourbons using rye can also be smooth, they generally have spicier notes to the flavor. The mash bill used for Pappy is the same as the one used for Weller, another bourbon made at Buffalo Trace; however, the real magic happens in the aging and blending process. Depending on how and where the barrels are aged and the proof the bourbon is bottled at, the end results can be entirely different.

If you look at the manufacturer's suggested retail prices (MSRPs) for five currently available Van Winkle bourbons and ryes, they are in line with other bourbons of the same age, availability, and history. A bottle of ten-year-old Rip Van Winkle should be in the $60 range, and a bottle of twenty-three-year-old Pappy Van Winkle Family Reserve should be about $270. This may seem a high price to pay, but you have to remember a filled fifty-three-gallon barrel may have fewer than ten gallons left after twenty-three years, thanks to the angel's share.

In some parts of the country, these prices may not be accurate as stores tend to mark it up due to the mystique and the people willing to pay ridiculous prices. A secondary market exists where people will resell bottles. I have heard of people asking for more than a 1,000 percent markup. Some retailers are seeing this and thinking they can get those same prices, but

thankfully it is rare to find this locally. Here in Louisville, most stores are raffling off the right to purchase the limited number of bottles they receive. This seems a fairer way to distribute the very limited number of bottles available to the large number of people who want to buy one.

In 2017, a new release was announced: a twenty-five-year-old Rip Van Winkle with an estimated MSRP of $1,800. This very limited edition has only about seven hundred bottles available.

It seemed as if people started lining up the moment it was announced.

Now for the big question: Is it worth it? Well, as with so many things, the answer is "it depends." Good bourbon is like good wine in that everyone has their own opinion of what's worth it. Everyone's taste is different and is constantly evolving. Some of my favorite bourbons are those I never liked when I first started drinking bourbon; at the same time, I've outgrown some of my old favorites as my palate evolved and I started to look for more complex flavors. Pappy's is really good, and I have enjoyed it many times. At the same time, there are a lot of great bourbons out there. I have a bottle of each Pappy's, and I enjoy the challenge of trying to find one every year—sometimes even twice a year.

Drink what you like and don't be afraid to splurge once in a while on something that not many people get to have anymore. The way it seems to be going, you never know when you will get another opportunity.

Fred Ruffenach

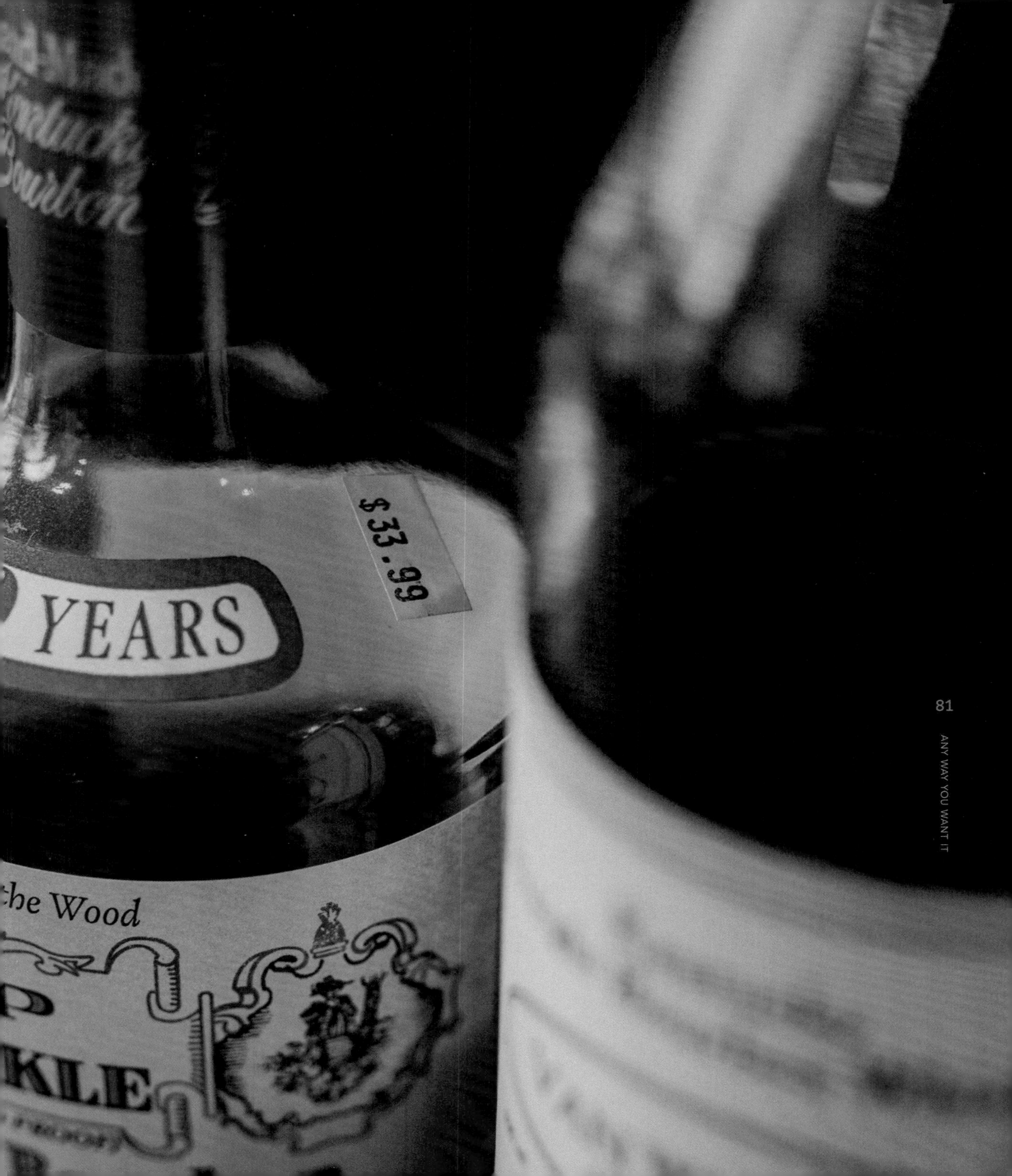
$33.99
YEARS
the Wood

Experiment

The best way to find out what you like is to experiment. Just like a cookie dough recipe, once you have a good base you can add the ingredients to create your own family-favorite recipe. Don't be afraid to experiment and try new things. Come up with your own favorite combinations and create your signature cocktail.

Classic Bourbon Highball

In a highball glass, add ice and 2 ounces of bourbon, fill with ginger ale, and stir.

Peach Vanilla Highball

Fill glass with ice, 2 ounces of bourbon, and 1 ounce peach vanilla syrup. Top with sparkling water and stir. Garnish with a slice of peach and sprig of mint (optional).

Classic Bourbon Manhattan Martini

In a large glass or cocktail shaker, add 2 ounces of bourbon and 1 ounce sweet vermouth. Add a dash or two of bitters. We use Angostura or Peychaud. Add ice and mix. Strain into a martini glass and add a maraschino cherry.

Kick It Up Apple Bourbon Martini

In a cocktail shaker add ice, 2 ounces of Maker's Mark bourbon, 1 ounce jalapeño apple syrup, and a splash of apple cider. Shake vigorously. Strain into a martini glass. Garnish with a slice of apple.

Strawberry Fields Old Fashioned

In a rocks glass, add 1 ounce of strawberry simple syrup and a dash of orange bitters, then add ice, filling about halfway. Add 2 ounces of bourbon. Stir until cold. Garnish with a strawberry and a piece of mint.

Pumpkin-Spiced Old Fashioned

In a rocks glass, add 1 ounce of pumpkin-spiced simple syrup and a dash of orange bitters, then add ice, filling about halfway. Add 2 ounces of bourbon. Stir until cold. Garnish with an orange or lemon twist and a piece of candied ginger.

Classic Mint Julep

Fill a julep cup with crushed ice. Add 2 ounces of bourbon and 1 ounce of mint julep simple syrup. Garnish with a sprig of mint and serve.

Strawberry Bourbon Lemonade with Rosemary

Fill a julep cup with crushed ice. Add 2 ounces of bourbon, 1 ounce of strawberry simple syrup, and 1 ounce lemonade. Garnish with a sprig of rosemary and serve.

Blackberry Basil Julep

Fill a julep cup with crushed ice. Add 2 ounces of bourbon and 1 ounce of blackberry basil julep simple syrup. Garnish with a sprig of fresh basil and blackberry and serve.

Bourbon Suppa Club

FIVE

Bourbon Suppa Club

If you have ever spent any time in the South or know anyone from the South, you have probably experienced that southern hospitality. And it's best exhibited through food and drink. Even as a young child I remember friends and family stopping by our house on the weekend, and the first thing my mother or father asked was, "Can I get you something to eat or drink?" If you knew my dad even a little bit, you knew to say yes right away because he would be relentless in his pursuit of providing you nutrition or a libation. Even as kids, we reveled in the hospitality, as we learned early on how to make the perfect highball or prepare small bites for company. For me, this tradition carried on into adulthood. I love to cook and entertain. The creative outlets of planning, preparing, and final presentation were a welcome respite from the corporate world in which I spent so much of my time. When I got married, besides sharing my life with a wonderful man, I was most excited about having someone to cook for every night.

Combine my love of bourbon, cooking, entertaining, and all things Kentucky, and you can imagine how excited I was to be asked to join the Bourbon Suppa Club. Monthly book clubs or bunko nights were never my thing. While I enjoyed the camaraderie of other women, I found being part of a book club created unnecessary added pressure. Reading became less about relaxation and more about trying to keep up with my smart friends on the latest Oprah-endorsed literary masterpiece. Bunko nights involved less pressure but I found myself making small talk with women I hardly knew, eating bad snacks, and walking away with a new prize for our next yard sale. Plus, I did not like playing dice games.

I met Velma, one of the founding members of the Bourbon Suppa Club, through the Whisky Chicks. I remember traveling next to her on a bus trip to the Maker's Mark distillery in Loretto, Kentucky. You could instantly tell that she was a confident woman who was passionate about bourbon. She had a strong fashion sense and is one of those rare women who can wear animal prints and make them look elegant. Her inner and outer beauty shined through. We instantly connected, and I knew that, given the chance, I would love to get to know her better. She shared with me about how

Two Whisky Chicks enjoying bourbon-spiked hot chocolate.

she and a group of girlfriends would get together once a month and experiment with different types of bourbons, creating unique cocktails and cooking five- to six-course meals centered around bourbon. I was immediately intrigued.

As things go, life got busy and Velma did not make it back to a Whisky Chicks event for a few months. When she joined us on a behind-the-scenes tour of Four Roses, she brought friends with her from the Bourbon Suppa Club. I was only able to spend a short amount of time with Velma that day, but we promised to get together for coffee in the next few weeks. I am thankful we both followed through and a new friendship was formed. I was thrilled when she asked me to become part of the group and invited me to my first dinner. The Suppa Club gets together the first Thursday of each month, each time at a different member's house. The hostess for the evening puts together a menu that includes a welcoming cocktail, an appetizer, salad, entrée, two side dishes, dessert, and an after-dinner cocktail. The most important requirement is that they all have to include bourbon. The hostess usually prepares the entrée and the other members take responsibility for one of the other recipes.

I didn't know what to expect my first night. I was a bit nervous about going to a stranger's home, sharing a meal with women I hardly knew. Being my father's daughter, I arrived five minutes early and decided I would drive around the neighborhood before knocking on the front door. When I showed up on Sarah P.'s doorstep, I was greeted by the hostess with a warm hug and a cocktail. The evening was off to a great start. As others arrived and introduced themselves, my anxiety began to diminish. That evening I enjoyed a fabulous meal with a new set of friends who have now become some of my favorite people to spend time with.

Being part of the Bourbon Suppa Club has been an incredible blessing, and you can easily do something like this with your friends too. It begins with finding recipes that include bourbon and compiling your first menu. This is where Pinterest and the hundreds of online blogs, food magazines, and old cookbooks lend inspiration. As a general rule, I scan a new recipe and then figure out ways to modify it to make it my own. The Bourbon Suppa Club members do the same thing, and the modification usually involves adding more bourbon. The menu below is composed of discovered recipes with simple changes to enhance the flavors to match my preferences.

My First Bourbon Suppa Club Menu

Aperitif—Bourbon Apple Cider

Appetizer—Flatbread with Bourbon Fig Jam, Crispy Prosciutto, Blue Cheese, and Arugula

Salad—Bourbon-Roasted Pear Salad with Gorgonzola, Bourbon-Spiced Candied Walnuts, and Bourbon Apple Cider Vinaigrette

Main Course—Bourbon Chicken

Warm Cornbread with Bourbon Maple Pecan Butter

Bourbon Bacon Brussels Sprouts with Apples

Dessert—Bourbon Pumpkin Pie with Bourbon Whipped Cream

After-Dinner Cocktail—Bourbon-Spiked Hot Chocolate

Bourbon Apple Cider Rimmed in Cinnamon Sugar

(MAKES 6–8 SERVINGS)

The evening started off with a simple, delicious cocktail that was perfect for a fall evening. The highlight was the glass rimmed in cinnamon sugar. Because it was equal parts cinnamon and sugar, the spiciness of the cinnamon gave it a nice little kick.

Ingredients:

2 tablespoons granulated sugar

2 tablespoons ground cinnamon

2 tablespoons, 2 cups apple cider, divided

1 cup bourbon

In a shallow bowl or on a plate, mix together granulated sugar and cinnamon. In a separate bowl, pour 2 tablespoons apple cider. Dip the rim of each glass in the apple cider and then into the cinnamon-sugar mixture.

In a separate ice-filled pitcher, combine bourbon and 2 cups apple cider. Stir together and serve. Garnish with a cinnamon stick, rosemary sprig, or slice of apple.

Flatbread with Bourbon Fig Jam, Crispy Prosciutto, Blue Cheese, and Arugula

Bourbon, bacon, cheese, and jam? Heck yeah! The crispiness of the prosciutto and the saltiness from the cheese combine with the bourbon-infused sweet fig jam to create the perfect balance for the palate.

Ingredients:

½ cup fig jam

1 tablespoon of your favorite bourbon (feel free to adjust based on your preference)

2 large pieces of flatbread pizza crust

2–3 tablespoons of blue cheese

2 ounces of thinly sliced prosciutto

1 cup chopped arugula

aged balsamic vinegar

Arrange prosciutto on a wire rack on a baking sheet. Crisp in 350° oven for 15 minutes. Set aside. Combine fig jam and bourbon in small bowl. Place flatbread on a sheet pan. Spread the fig jam mixture on the flatbread, and top with blue cheese. Top with the crisped prosciutto.

Bake in preheated 350° oven for 8–10 minutes or until cheese begins to melt. Remove from oven and top with arugula. Drizzle with aged balsamic vinegar. Cut into squares and serve.

My contribution for the night was the salad course. This salad is a bit more complicated than I would generally make, but the individual components are easy to prepare and are delicious on their own. Add a protein and this salad could be your main course.

Bourbon-Roasted Pear Salad with Gorgonzola, Bourbon-Spiced Candied Walnuts, and Bourbon Apple Cider Vinaigrette

(MAKES 6–8 SERVINGS)

Ingredients:

16 ounces spring salad mix

8 bourbon-roasted pear halves

1 cup Gorgonzola

1 cup bourbon-spiced candied walnuts

¾ cup pomegranate arils

Place spring salad mix in a large bowl. Cut each bourbon-roasted pear half into 4 pieces and arrange on top of salad. Sprinkle with Gorgonzola, bourbon-spiced candied walnuts, and pomegranate arils. Top salad with Bourbon Apple Cider Vinaigrette and toss.

Bourbon-Spiced Candied Walnuts

Ingredients:

4 tablespoons butter

2 cups walnut halves

2 tablespoons brown sugar

1 teaspoon bourbon

1 teaspoon Cajun seasoning

In a skillet combine butter and walnut halves. Over medium heat, stir for about 2–3 minutes until walnuts begin to toast. Add brown sugar, bourbon, and Cajun seasoning. Cook on low heat for 1–2 minutes or until sugar melts. Transfer to a parchment-paper-lined baking sheet, spread into a single layer, and let cool.

Bourbon-Roasted Pears

Ingredients:

4 Bosc pears

Salt and pepper

1 tablespoon olive oil

¼ cup of bourbon

1 tablespoon brown sugar

Preheat oven to 350°. Cut pears in half and core, leaving skin on. Sprinkle with salt and pepper. Heat up a large ovenproof skillet (I used my grandmother's iron skillet), and drizzle it with olive oil. Place the pears facedown in the skillet and brown for 3–4 minutes. Turn the pears over and deglaze the pan with bourbon. Then sprinkle pears with brown sugar. Place the pan in the oven, and roast pears for 10 minutes or until they are soft enough to pierce easily with a fork. Remove from pan and let cool.

Can be prepared and refrigerated a day ahead of time.

Bourbon Apple Cider Vinaigrette

Ingredients:

¼ cup apple cider vinegar

2 tablespoons apple cider

1 tablespoon bourbon

1 tablespoon minced shallot

Pinch of salt

½ tablespoon minced fresh herbs (we use a house blend of thyme, rosemary, and sage)

½ teaspoon freshly ground pepper

⅓ cup olive oil

Whisk together apple cider vinegar, apple cider, bourbon, minced shallot, minced fresh herbs, salt, and ground pepper. Continue whisking and add olive oil. (I sometimes lighten things up by using a little less oil. You can always add more.)

Bourbon Chicken

The bourbon-inspired entrée for the evening was a variation on the bourbon chicken you might sample when walking through the food court of your favorite mall. The added kick of the bourbon and the spice was a great complement to the rest of the meal. The best part is that it only takes five minutes of hands-on work to prepare this dish. Be sure to leave time to marinate the chicken for at least four hours, preferably overnight.

Ingredients:

¼ cup olive oil

½ cup low-sodium soy sauce

¼ cup apple cider vinegar

¼ cup bourbon

¼ cup brown sugar

1 tablespoon crushed or finely chopped ginger

2 tablespoons crushed garlic

1 tablespoon Sriracha sauce

½ teaspoon red pepper flakes

2 pounds sliced chicken breasts or tenders

In a large bowl combine olive oil, low-sodium soy sauce, apple cider vinegar, bourbon, brown sugar, ginger, garlic, Sriracha sauce, and red pepper flakes. Arrange chicken in a shallow baking dish. Top with marinade and combine. Cover and refrigerate for at least 4 hours; best if left overnight.

Preheat oven to 350°, uncover chicken, and bake in marinade for 30–45 minutes, turning and basting periodically. When chicken is done, heat under broiler for another 5 minutes to form sticky caramelized top. Serve over rice.

Bourbon Maple Pecan Butter

My favorite bite of the night was the cornbread with bourbon maple pecan butter. Like most of the other dishes, it is easy to prepare and packs a wallop of flavor.

Ingredients:

1 stick softened butter

2 tablespoons chopped pecans

1 tablespoon maple syrup

1 tablespoon of bourbon

Combine all ingredients. Serve with cornbread, muffins, pancakes, waffles, or as desired. Keep refrigerated until ready to serve.

Bourbon Bacon Brussels Sprouts with Apples

Brussels sprouts have become one of my favorite vegetables, especially when they are combined with a little bit of bacon and apple. This is a dish we serve every Thanksgiving.

Ingredients:

2–3 pounds Brussels sprouts, trimmed, cleaned, and each cut in half

½ pound chopped bacon

¼ cup sweet onions

½ cup chopped apple (1 medium Granny Smith apple)

½ cup bourbon

½ cup apple cider

1 tablespoon brown sugar

Salt and pepper

In a large skillet, brown the bacon. Remove bacon and grease from pan, leaving a little fat behind. Add onions and apples to skillet and brown. Deglaze the pan by adding bourbon, apple cider, and brown sugar. Bring to a boil and then stir in the Brussels sprouts, coating thoroughly. Add salt and pepper to taste. Reduce heat, cover, and let simmer 30 minutes or until tender. Sprinkle with bacon right before serving.

Did someone say dessert? Bourbon pairs well with so many different desserts, which makes it a great addition to some of your all-time favorites, like this Bourbon Pumpkin Pie. If you don't like the idea of messing with Grandma's recipe but want to kick things up a bit, try the Bourbon Whipped Cream as a topping for your favorite sweet. It is a decadent addition to the Chocolate Bourbon Pecan Pie on page 20.

Bourbon Pumpkin Pie

Ingredients:

2 large eggs

1 can pumpkin puree

¾ cup packed light brown sugar

2 teaspoons pumpkin pie spice

Pinch of salt

12-ounce can evaporated milk

3 tablespoons bourbon

Prepared piecrust

Preheat oven to 425°. In a large bowl combine eggs, pumpkin puree, brown sugar, pumpkin pie spice, and salt. Add evaporated milk and bourbon. Pour mixture into prepared, unbaked piecrust. Bake for 15 minutes then reduce oven temperature to 350° degrees and bake for an additional 40–50 minutes until custard is set. Cool on wire rack for 2 hours and then refrigerate. When ready to serve, top with bourbon whipped cream.

Bourbon Whipped Cream

Ingredients:

1 cup heavy whipping cream

2 tablespoons powdered sugar

1 tablespoon bourbon

½ teaspoon vanilla extract

In a large mixing bowl combine whipping cream, powdered sugar, bourbon, and vanilla extract. Using an electric mixer, beat until soft peaks are formed. Refrigerate and serve with favorite dessert or atop your favorite hot beverage. Feel free to adjust the amount of powdered sugar and bourbon to match your flavor preference.

Bourbon-Spiked Hot Chocolate

(MAKES 4 SERVINGS)

What better way to finish a wonderful dinner than with a delicious warm cocktail made with bourbon and chocolate? This hot chocolate is the perfect treat for you and your favorite someone to share next to a cozy fire on chilly winter nights.

Ingredients:

⅓ cup cocoa powder

½ cup sugar

Dash of salt

⅓ cup water

3 cups milk

1 teaspoon vanilla

Half and half

8 tablespoons bourbon

Marshmallows

In a bowl, combine cocoa powder, sugar, and salt. In a medium saucepan bring water to a boil. Add dry mixture, stirring until the sugar and cocoa have dissolved and the mixture is combined thoroughly. Stir in milk and vanilla. Turn heat down to medium, letting the milk heat up to preferred drinking temperature. Fill each mug three-quarters full and add a splash of half and half and 2 tablespoons bourbon. Stir. Top with marshmallows and serve immediately.

For an added effect, you may lightly toast or brulee the marshmallows with a small kitchen torch until golden brown.

101

Sunday Brunch

One of my favorite memories from my childhood was coming home after church and having a humongous breakfast. Each week there would be a different selection of treats, including waffles or pancakes with warm syrup, southern biscuits with sausage gravy, or homemade German kuchen pastry. Preparation seemed to take forever, but the wait was always well worth it when we all sat down and enjoyed a decadent meal together. Because of the abundance of food and the richness of the selections, many times it was the only meal we ate that day. After I grew older and moved away, breakfast on the weekends remained a sacred indulgence. To this day, Sunday brunch at our house is an honored tradition that has expanded to include many bourbon-related treats.

This recommended menu is a combination of my favorite brunch items and a brunch inspired by a Bourbon Suppa Club get-together.

Every Day Is a Good Day for a Bourbon Brunch

Cocktails—Maple Bourbon Coffee, Bourbon Bloody Mary, Blood Orange Bourbon Mimosa

Brunch Buffet—Apple Cranberry Pancakes (Gluten Free) with Bourbon Maple Syrup

Bourbon-Glazed Bacon

Sautéed Green Beans with Garlic and Bourbon

Roasted Sweet Potatoes with Bourbon Maple Pecan Butter

Bourbon Corn Pudding with Maple Bourbon Candied Jalapeños

Bourbon-Macerated Berries

Jalapeño Cornbread Biscuits with Bacon Bourbon Jam (Gluten Free)

Baked Eggs with Broccoli, Spinach, Mushrooms, Peppers, and Onions

Bourbon Banana Cake

A brunch is not complete without coffee, Bloody Marys, and Mimosas. I wasn't surprised to discover that all three are even more delicious when made with Kentucky bourbon.

Maple Bourbon Coffee

Ingredients:

Hot coffee

1 tablespoon bourbon

1 tablespoon half and half

1 tablespoon maple syrup

Whipped cream and brown sugar (or bourbon sugar), for garnish

Fill a mug about halfway with hot coffee. Add bourbon, half and half, and maple syrup.

Stir together. Top with whipped cream and sprinkles of brown sugar or bourbon sugar.

Bourbon Bloody Mary

Ingredients:

Ice

1 ounce bourbon

4 ounces tomato juice

Dash of Worcestershire sauce

¼ teaspoon fresh horseradish

2–3 dashes of hot sauce (I use Valentina Red Label)

Pinch of celery salt

Pinch of bourbon-smoked black pepper

Fill a tall glass with ice. Add bourbon, tomato juice, Worcestershire sauce, horseradish, hot sauce, celery salt, and black pepper. Stir together and garnish with a celery stick and banana pepper.

Optional: Rim the glass with lemon and dip into *togarashi* (a peppery Japanese condiment).

Blood Orange Bourbon Mimosa

Ingredients:

Ice

2 ounces bourbon

½ cup freshly squeezed blood orange juice

1 teaspoon agave or maple syrup

Prosecco or sparkling wine

Mint sprigs, for garnish *(optional)*

Fill a cocktail shaker with ice. Add bourbon, blood orange juice, and agave or maple syrup.

Mix together vigorously until chilled. Strain and fill two champagne glasses halfway. Add prosecco or sparkling wine. Garnish with a sprig of mint if desired.

The mouthwatering combination of apples, cranberries, and bourbon adds a delectable flavor to any breakfast table. When served with bacon and bourbon maple syrup, it creates the right balance between sweet and savory.

Apple Cranberry Pancakes with Bourbon Maple Syrup (Gluten-Free)

Ingredients:

¼ cup chopped dried apples

¼ cup chopped dried cranberries

1 tablespoon bourbon

Your favorite pancake batter or:

1 cup Pamela's Gluten-Free Baking & Pancake Mix

1 ¼ cups milk

1 egg

Dash of cinnamon

In a bowl combine dried apples, dried cranberries, and bourbon. Let sit for 30 minutes and then drain excess bourbon (I don't believe in wasting bourbon so I like to set it aside and use in a cocktail later).

Create a basic pancake batter mix using your favorite recipe, or mix Pamela's Gluten-Free Baking & Pancake Mix, milk, egg, and cinnamon.

Heat a lightly oiled griddle or frying pan over medium high heat. Pour the batter onto the griddle, using about ¼ cup for each pancake. Before flipping to cook the other side, top each with a mix of apples and cranberries. Cook until golden brown. Top with Bourbon Maple Syrup.

Bourbon Maple Syrup

Ingredients:

¼ cup butter

1 ½ cups maple syrup

1–2 tablespoons bourbon

In a medium saucepan combine butter and maple syrup. Bring to a boil, turn off heat, and add bourbon. Serve over pancakes. This syrup is also delicious in cocktails!

Bourbon-Glazed Bacon

Who doesn't love bacon? I have seen this simple and extremely popular side item served as a stand-alone appetizer. It is a fabulous addition to a salad, or it can be used as a garnish for your favorite deviled egg recipe.

Ingredients:

3 tablespoons brown sugar

½ teaspoon Cajun seasoning, such as Zatarains

3 tablespoons maple syrup

2 tablespoons bourbon

1 pound bacon

In a large bowl combine brown sugar, Cajun seasoning, maple syrup, and bourbon. Add bacon, separating each slice and then tossing it in the mixture to get an even coat. Line a baking sheet with foil, arranging bacon in a flat, even layer. Bake at 350° for 25–30 minutes or until crispy. Let cool for 5 minutes before serving.

Sautéed Green Beans with Garlic and Bourbon

My husband invented this dish by accident, sans the bourbon. He was making me dinner one night and ended up cooking the garlic a little too long. What we discovered is that it created the amazing smoky flavor of bacon without all of the fat. Using bourbon to deglaze the pan adds that little extra touch at the end, though this step is optional.

Ingredients:

1 tablespoon olive oil

1 tablespoon butter

1 tablespoon finely chopped garlic

1 pound fresh green beans with ends removed

1 tablespoon bourbon

In a large sauté pan add olive oil, butter, and garlic. Sauté until the garlic begins to caramelize and turn slightly brown. Add green beans. Continue to stir until garlic starts to turn darker brown and green beans are tender. Remove green beans from the pan, and add bourbon to deglaze the pan. Pour over top of green beans and serve.

Roasted Sweet Potatoes with Bourbon Maple Pecan Butter

Here is another way to use the Bourbon Maple Pecan Butter. This simple recipe is a delightful addition to your fall lineup or, in this case, brunch buffet.

Ingredients:

2 tablespoons olive oil

½ teaspoon cinnamon

½ teaspoon cayenne pepper

Dash of salt

Dash of bourbon-smoked pepper

4 medium sweet potatoes, peeled and sliced into half-inch rounds

6 tablespoons Bourbon Maple Pecan Butter (*page 97*)

Preheat oven to 400°. In a large bowl combine olive oil, cinnamon, cayenne pepper, salt, and bourbon-smoked pepper. Add sweet potatoes and toss until evenly coated. Arrange on a foil-lined baking sheet. Roast on one side for 20 minutes, flip, and roast another 20 minutes.

Meanwhile, melt 6 tablespoons of Bourbon Maple Pecan Butter in a small saucepan. Remove sweet potatoes from the oven and smash each one slightly with a spoon. Drizzle each potato with a bit of the melted pecan butter and return to oven for 5 minutes. Serve warm.

Bourbon-Macerated Berries

This recipe can be used for berries as well as other fresh fruits like melons and grapes.

Ingredients:

2 tablespoons lime juice

2 tablespoons honey

2 tablespoons of bourbon

3 cups any combination of fresh berries (I like raspberries, blackberries, and strawberries)

1 sprig fresh mint, chopped

In a bowl combine lime juice, honey, and bourbon. Add berries. Add freshly chopped mint and stir. Let sit for about 20 minutes and serve. Leftovers can be used to create a delicious cobbler cocktail by mashing the fruit and adding sparkling water and a little more bourbon.

I have always been a big fan of sweet and savory, and I get even more excited when there is a little heat thrown in. The added bonus is that when it comes straight from the oven, the aroma is reminiscent of the sweet corn mash cooking at a distillery.

Bourbon Corn Pudding with Maple Bourbon Candied Jalapeños

Ingredients:

1 8-ounce package of cream cheese softened

2 eggs

6 tablespoons butter melted

¼ cup honey

1 cup cornmeal

½ teaspoon salt

½ teaspoon pepper

⅓ cup bourbon

1 ½ cups milk

4 cups fresh or frozen corn

1 cup sharp cheddar cheese grated

Preheat the oven to 350°. Grease a 9 × 3–inch baking dish.

In a large mixing bowl, beat together cream cheese, eggs, melted butter, and honey. Add cornmeal, salt, pepper, and bourbon. Slowly add in the milk, mixing all of the ingredients together to create a thick batter. Add the corn and blend together for an additional 2 minutes, breaking up the kernels of corn to release their natural juices. Fold in the cheese.

Pour into prepared pan. Bake for 45–55 minutes until it is slightly golden on top and the center is set. Let sit for 10 minutes before serving.

Maple Bourbon Candied Jalapeños

Ingredients:

½ cup light brown sugar

½ pure maple syrup

1 cup unfiltered apple cider

½ cup bourbon

Pinch of salt

8 fresh jalapeños sliced

Combine brown sugar, maple syrup, apple cider, bourbon, and salt in a medium sauce pan. Over high heat dissolve the sugar and bring to a boil. Turn heat down to medium low and boil for an additional 3–4 minutes until liquid begins to thicken slightly.

Add sliced jalapeños and cook for an additional 3–4 minutes. Remove from heat and let cool. Store in a sealed glass container in the refrigerator for up to 4 weeks.

This is the only recipe that does not contain bourbon, but I could not resist. The first time I had a version of this recipe was at a Bourbon Suppa Club. It was the base for a Hot Brown (an open-faced sandwich dish native to Louisville, Kentucky, that is topped with turkey, mornay sauce, bacon, and tomato). It is the perfect match for the Bacon Bourbon Jam and goes well with the Bourbon Maple Pecan Butter (page 97). Because my husband has to eat gluten free, I have modified the recipe using Pamela's Gluten-Free Baking & Pancake Mix and gluten-free cornmeal. You can always use self-rising flour in its place.

Jalapeño Cornbread Biscuits
(Gluten-Free)

Ingredients:

1 egg

¾ cup buttermilk

¼ cup honey

1 ½ cups Pamela's Gluten-Free Pancake & Baking Mix

1 ½ cups gluten-free cornmeal

2 tablespoons baking powder

½ teaspoon salt

½ teaspoon bourbon-smoked pepper

¾ cup cold butter

¾ cup sharp cheddar cheese, grated

2 finely diced jalapeños (seeds removed)

Preheat oven to 400°. Whisk together egg, buttermilk, and honey. Set aside.

In a large mixing bowl combine Pamela's Gluten-Free Pancake & Baking Mix, gluten-free cornmeal, baking powder, salt, and bourbon-smoked pepper. Chop cold butter into small cubes. Either by hand or with a pastry blender, mix into dry ingredients, creating coarse crumbles. Slowly stir in wet mixture until just combined. Be careful not to overmix. Fold in cheddar cheese and jalapeños.

Using an ice cream scoop, drop batter on a non-stick sheet pan, leaving room for the biscuits to expand slightly. Brush with melted butter or buttermilk. Bake at 350° for 15–20 minutes or until golden brown.

Bacon Bourbon Jam

Ingredients:

1 pound chopped uncooked bacon

2 cups chopped onions (2 medium onions)

1 tablespoon chopped garlic

¼ cup apple cider vinegar

½ cup brown sugar

¼ cup of bourbon

In a skillet, brown bacon until slightly crisp. Remove bacon from pan and let rest on paper towels to drain the fat. Discard most of bacon grease, keeping approximately 3 tablespoons in the skillet. Add onions and garlic to the skillet and cook for about 5 minutes until onions are soft and translucent. Add apple cider vinegar, brown sugar, and bourbon to the skillet.

Bring to a boil and let cook for 3–4 minutes. Add bacon. Turn down the heat and let simmer until most of the liquid evaporates and the remainder comes to a jam consistency. Serve with cornbread or on sandwiches. Store in airtight container in the refrigerator for up to a month.

Baked Eggs with Broccoli, Spinach, Mushrooms, Peppers, and Onions

(MAKES 6 SERVINGS)

I have always loved the combination of broccoli, spinach, mushrooms, onions, and peppers. I remember being in my first apartment and learning to cook for one person. The variety of dishes I created using this classic medley of veggies ranged from quesadillas, omelets, and paninis to nachos and pizza. This dish is an easy way to serve eggs to a bigger crowd and provides a healthy addition to an otherwise decadent meal. It's also a great way to use up those little bits of leftover veggies in the refrigerator. Of course we kicked up the flavor with a splash of bourbon.

Ingredients:

2 tablespoons olive oil

1 teaspoon red pepper flakes

¼ cup chopped broccoli

¼ cup mushrooms

1 cup chopped fresh spinach

¼ cup chopped onions

¼ cup chopped red bell pepper

2 teaspoons of bourbon (optional)

6 eggs

Parmesan cheese

Preheat oven to 350°. In a large sauté pan heat olive oil and red pepper flakes. Add broccoli, mushrooms, spinach, onions, and red bell pepper. Sauté until veggies are tender and onions are slightly caramelized (just beginning to brown). In the last few minutes of cooking, add 2 teaspoons of bourbon (optional) to deglaze the pan.

Divide mixture up into 6 ramekins that have been sprayed with cooking spray, and place them on a cooking sheet. Crack a raw egg into each ramekin. Place in the oven and bake eggs until desired doneness (10–12 minutes). Sprinkle with shredded Parmesan cheese and serve.

Bourbon Banana Cake
(Gluten-Free)

It was another lazy weekend at home. I was feeling a little bored, so I decided to peruse the Internet looking for a spark of creativity. There were four ripe bananas on the counter, and my sweet tooth was calling. Since my husband is gluten free, I had to get creative.

Ingredients:

For the topping

¾ cup of melted butter

2 tablespoons of bourbon

¾ cup brown sugar

3–4 sliced ripe bananas

Preheat oven to 350°. Spray a 9-inch springform pan with cooking spray.

In a small bowl, combine the butter, bourbon, and brown sugar. Pour into springform pan. Arrange the banana slices in a single layer. Set aside.

For the cake

⅔ cup butter softened

2 eggs

1 cup white sugar

1 tablespoon bourbon

4 ounces cream cheese

¼ cup milk

2 cups of Pamela's Gluten Free Baking & Pancake Mix

(may be substituted with 2 cups all-purpose flour, 2 teaspoons baking powder, and ½ teaspoon baking soda)

In a large mixing bowl, cream together butter, eggs, and sugar. Mix in bourbon, cream cheese, milk, and flour mixture until well blended. Batter should be light and fluffy. Gently add batter evenly over the top of the bananas.

I recommend placing the springform pan on a baking sheet in the event of leakage or overflow. Bake at 350° for 40–45 minutes. It should be golden brown, and an inserted toothpick should come out clean. Remove from oven and let cool for at least 1 hour.

Release from springform pan and invert onto a platter. Carefully take a butter knife around the edge of the bottom of the springform pan to loosen the base, gently removing the cake. The cake should resemble a pineapple upside down cake but with bananas. Slice and serve as is or add a bit of bourbon caramel sauce.

When it was my turn to host, of course I wanted to come up with a menu that would impress and wow but that also included simple recipes that were fun to make. My husband loves to show off and share his extensive bourbon collection. What we came up with was an assortment of appetizers that we paired with different bourbons from our personal collection.

Hopefully, these recipes for food and bourbon will pique your taste buds and inspire you to create a menu for your own Bourbon Suppa Club. Remember, it doesn't have to be fancy, just fun. The idea is to celebrate new friendships, enjoy old ones, and create memories with every event. Cheers!

Small Bites

Bourbon Candied Bacon Deviled Eggs

Kale Salad with Bourbon Balsamic Dressing

Bourbon Five-Spice Apples

Krispy Kreme Bourbon Barbecue Pork Sliders

Bourbon Street Shrimp

Bourbon Mushrooms with Caramelized Onion Polenta Bites

Flourless Chocolate Brownies with Bourbon Sea Salt and Bourbon Smoked Sugar

Classic Manhattan with Homemade Luxardo Cherries

Bourbon Candied Bacon Deviled Eggs

Every Christmas Eve, Aunt Mary Catherine would host the entire extended family at her house. I recall looking forward to this night every year, not just because it was the night before Christmas but because it was a night full of spectacular food. My Aunt M. C. (as I liked to call her) was rarely seen without a cocktail in one hand and a cigarette in the other. She was the original Whisky Chick and is partially responsible for my love of entertaining. Each family would be asked to bring an appetizer, and my mother was always nominated to bring the deviled eggs, which was her least favorite thing to make. Over the years, the responsibility was delegated to me, and this modified recipe is inspired by Aunt M. C. It is a little bit salty and sweet just like her.

Ingredients:

6 eggs, hardboiled

¼ cup light mayonnaise

1 tablespoon Dijon mustard

1 tablespoon Sriracha sauce

Pinch of salt

Pinch of bourbon-smoked pepper

Peel eggs and cut lengthwise. Remove yolks into mixing bowl and add mayonnaise, Dijon mustard, Sriracha sauce, salt, and bourbon-smoked pepper. Smash and blend mixture with a fork until smooth and creamy. Spoon or use a pastry bag to pipe into egg white halves. Top each with one dot of Sriracha sauce and a piece of Bourbon-Glazed Bacon (page 106). Refrigerate until ready to serve.

Kale Salad with Bourbon Balsamic Dressing

Kale is one of the hardiest greens available. It is built to survive the winter. Until it became trendy, it was traditionally sautéed to make greens or used as a vegetable in stews. Using kale in salad has become very popular, but to be successful it needs to be treated with extra care and attention, including gently massaging it before serving. Yes, kale is best after a quick rubdown, which allows this tough green to soften and become easier to eat.

Ingredients:

¼ cup dried cherries

1 tablespoon bourbon

1 pound chopped Tuscan leafy kale (stems removed)

Prepared Bourbon Balsamic Dressing

¼ cup blue cheese

¼ cup chopped Spicy Bourbon Pecans

In a small bowl combine dried cherries with bourbon. Let sit for at least an hour.

In a large bowl, combine kale and Bourbon Balsamic Dressing. With your hands, massage the kale, blending it with the dressing for 4–5 minutes. Top with blue cheese, cherries, and Spicy Bourbon Pecans. Toss just before serving.

Works great as a make-ahead salad. Serve in individual bowls or glasses.

Bourbon Balsamic Dressing

Ingredients:

2 tablespoons minced shallots

1 tablespoon minced garlic

¼ cup balsamic vinegar

2 tablespoons bourbon

½ teaspoon salt

¼ teaspoon pepper

1 tablespoon honey

⅔ cup extra virgin olive oil

In a small bowl combine shallots, garlic, balsamic vinegar, and bourbon. Whisk in salt, pepper, and honey. Slowly add olive oil until thoroughly blended.

Spicy Bourbon Pecans

Ingredients:

½ cup brown sugar

½ teaspoon salt

¼ teaspoon cayenne pepper

1 egg white

1 tablespoon bourbon

3 cups pecan halves

Preheat oven to 350°. In a small bowl, mix together brown sugar, salt, and cayenne pepper. Set aside.

In a medium bowl, whisk egg white until it becomes light and fluffy. Fold in bourbon and pecan halves. Once pecans have been coated evenly with egg white mixture, sprinkle with sugar mixture. Spread evenly on a cookie sheet lined with parchment paper. Bake for 20 minutes, stirring every 8–10 minutes. Remove from oven and let cool. Store in an airtight container.

Bourbon Five-Spice Apples

This dish was inspired by a five-spice pork dish that was served alongside cooked apples. Five-spice powder is a spice mixture used in Chinese cuisine. While there are many variants, the one used for this recipe was a blend of cinnamon, star anise, fennel, ginger, and cloves. I was amazed how well the ingredients melded together to deliver an explosive umami (savory) flavor.

Ingredients:

1 stick of butter

¼ cup dried cranberries

5–6 large Granny Smith apples peeled and sliced

2 teaspoons of five-spice powder

½ cup apple juice

½ cup maple syrup

2 tablespoons of lemon juice

½ cup of bourbon, divided

In a large skillet on medium heat combine butter, cranberries, apples, and five-spice powder. Coat the apples with the butter mixture until slightly warm, about 2–3 minutes. Add apple juice, maple syrup, lemon, and ¼ cup of bourbon.

Let simmer for a few minutes until the apples begin to soften. Remove apples from the pan, leaving the juices behind. Continue to cook juices on medium heat until it begins to cook down and thicken. Add the remaining ¼ cup of bourbon and light the pan with an open flame to cook off the alcohol, forming a glaze. Pour glaze over top of cooked apples. Best served warm.

Krispy Kreme Bourbon Barbecue Pork Sliders

When I first started my consulting and marketing business, we stumbled on the most amazing office space, located right on Whiskey Row in downtown Louisville. The open concept loft not only was perfect for our growing operation but also made an ideal location for parties. When we hosted our first open house, we decided to go with a carnival theme, preparing all kinds of finger foods that you might find at a state fair or carnival. After scouring ideas and recipes, I came up with this unique combination of pork barbecue and Krispy Kreme doughnuts. These bite-sized appetizers are fun to make, and they were a major hit at the party.

Ingredients:

3 dozen original Krispy Kreme glazed doughnut holes

3 cups pulled pork

1 cup prepared Bourbon Barbecue Sauce

Optional: Coleslaw, pickles

Split doughnut holes in half to form a small bun. In a bowl, combine pulled pork and Bourbon Barbecue Sauce. Place a spoonful of warm pulled pork on top of one half of each split doughnut hole. Top with the other half of donut and secure with toothpick.

Optional: Top pork with tablespoon of your favorite coleslaw or your favorite bread and butter pickle.

Simple Pulled Pork

Ingredients:

4-pound pork shoulder roast

2 tablespoons bourbon-smoked paprika

2 teaspoons salt

1 teaspoon bourbon-smoked pepper

1 tablespoon brown sugar

1 teaspoon cayenne pepper

1 teaspoon garlic powder

1 teaspoon onion powder

1 cup apple juice

Place a pork shoulder roast in a large slow cooker. In a small bowl, mix together bourbon-smoked paprika, salt, bourbon-smoked pepper, brown sugar, cayenne pepper, garlic powder, and onion powder. Rub pork roast with dry mixture. Add apple juice. Cover and cook on low for 8 hours. Remove pork from slow cooker, leaving behind juices and fat. Pull apart and shred the meat using two forks.

Simple Bourbon Barbecue Sauce

Ingredients:

Your favorite barbecue sauce

1 tablespoon Sriracha sauce

¼ cup favorite bourbon

Pour barbecue sauce in a large bowl. (I prefer Sweet Baby Ray's Sweet and Spicy Barbecue Sauce.) Add Sriracha sauce and bourbon. Stir together. Adjust the bourbon and Sriracha based on your personal taste preference.

Whiskey Row

Whiskey Row was the prime spot for the whiskey business in the late 1800s.
At its peak, there were close to ninety different brands located along the strip of Main Street in downtown Louisville, including Old Forester, Evan Williams, Bonnie Brothers Rye, Weller, J. T. S. Brown, and Four Roses. The reason for this was the proximity to the Ohio River. A full barrel averages five hundred pounds in weight, and the location of Whiskey Row made it easy to roll them downhill and onto a boat for transport. There were no distilleries operating on the strip of Main Street, rather they were scattered through the surrounding counties. Many brands had offices, warehouses, and bottling operations based on the street, however, which made access to financial centers and governing bodies convenient as well.

Today Whiskey Row is experiencing a revitalization and a return to its roots. Along Main Street you will find the official starting point for the Kentucky Bourbon Trail® adventure and the Kentucky Bourbon Trail Craft Tour® at the Frazier Museum. Whiskey Row of the twenty-first century will include Michter's, Evan Williams, Old Forester, Kentucky Peerless Distilling Company, and Angel's Envy.

Bourbon Street Shrimp

I met my husband in New Orleans, forever creating a bond to a city that we both love. This dish takes us back to Bourbon Street and fond memories of the early days of our relationship. We recommend serving this with a crunchy French bread so that not a single drop of the delicious sauce goes to waste.

Ingredients:

1 pound fresh uncooked shrimp, peeled and deveined.

1–2 tablespoons of your favorite Cajun seasoning (depending on preferred spice preference)

1 teaspoon bourbon-smoked pepper

1 stick butter

3 tablespoons bourbon

2 tablespoons Worcestershire sauce

2 tablespoons brown sugar

¼ cup fresh lemon juice

¼ cup chopped parsley

¼ cup chopped green onion

Preheat oven to 375°. Pat shrimp dry and spread out in a shallow 8 × 8–inch baking dish. Coat shrimp on both sides with Cajun seasoning. Sprinkle with bourbon-smoked pepper.

In a small saucepan melt butter and add bourbon, Worcestershire sauce, brown sugar, and lemon juice. Cook on low until sugar dissolves and sauce begins to thicken slightly. Pour over shrimp. Top with parsley and green onion. Bake for 12–15 minutes and serve.

Bourbon Mushrooms with Caramelized Onion Polenta Bites

The components for this elegant appetizer can be made ahead of time and assembled right before serving. The earthiness of the mushrooms and the sweetness of the caramelized onions pair well with the bourbon, creating an umami flavor. The polenta base provides a delicious gluten-free alternative for a bite-sized canapé. You can make your own polenta, which is fairly easy, or you can take the easier option, which we have done here, and use the ready-made polenta available in most grocery or specialty food stores.

Ingredients:

2 tablespoons olive oil, divided

1 teaspoon chopped garlic

8 ounces thinly sliced white mushrooms

Pinch of salt

Pinch of bourbon-smoked pepper

2 tablespoons bourbon

1 tablespoon butter

2 medium sweet yellow onions, sliced extra thin

1 bay leaf

1 tablespoon fresh thyme

Pinch of salt

1 18-ounce roll of polenta

In a large sauté pan, heat 1 tablespoon olive oil and garlic. Add mushrooms, salt, and bourbon-smoked pepper. Cook until mushrooms begin to soften and turn brown, about 3–4 minutes. Add bourbon to deglaze the pan. Continue to cook mushrooms for 2–3 minutes longer. Remove mushrooms from pan.

To the same pan, add remaining olive oil and the butter. Add onions, bay leaf, thyme, and salt. Spread onions out evenly in pan, stirring occasionally. Cook until they begin to turn golden brown. Discard bay leaf and remove from heat.

To prepare the polenta bites, slice polenta into quarter-inch round slices. Spread out on a parchment-lined cookie sheet. Bake at 375° for 10–15 minutes until slightly browned. Remove from oven and top with a small spoonful of caramelized onions and a small spoonful of mushrooms. Top with fresh thyme and serve.

Flourless Chocolate Brownies with Bourbon Sea Salt and Bourbon Smoked Sugar

No bourbon-inspired event is complete without a sweet ending, and you can't go wrong with chocolate. The richness of these brownies, made even more mouthwatering with the addition of bourbon-smoked sea salt, is the perfect pairing for your favorite bourbon on the rocks.

Ingredients:

Cooking spray

¾ cup semisweet chocolate chips

½ cup (1 stick) butter

¾ cup sugar

2 tablespoons bourbon

3 eggs

½ cup sifted cocoa

For the glaze:

¼ cup semisweet chocolate chips

1 ½ tablespoons butter

1 ½ teaspoons milk

1 ½ teaspoons honey

1 tablespoon bourbon

2 teaspoons bourbon-smoked sea salt

2 teaspoons bourbon-smoked sugar or coarse Demerara (large-crystal raw) sugar.

Preheat oven to 350°. Spray an 8 × 8–inch pan with cooking spray and line the bottom with parchment paper.

In a small saucepan on low heat, melt together chocolate chips and butter. Add sugar. Stir on low heat until sugar melts. Blend in bourbon. Remove from heat and whisk in eggs one by one, until fully blended. Add cocoa. Blend until the batter is smooth. Pour into your prepared pan and bake for 25–35 minutes. The center of the cake will be slightly firm but not hard. Be careful not to overbake.

For the glaze, melt together chocolate chips and butter. Once melted, remove from heat and add milk, honey, and bourbon. Stir until smooth and glossy. Once cake is fully cooled, pour glaze in the middle of the cake and spread evenly over the cake. Refrigerate for at least two hours.

In a separate bowl, mix together bourbon-smoked sea salt and bourbon-smoked sugar. When you are ready to serve, slide a knife around the sides of the pan and cut into small squares. Dip the glazed side of each brownie into the sugar-salt mixture and serve.

Classic Manhattan with Homemade Luxardo Cherries

Ingredients:

Ice

2 ounces bourbon

1 ounce sweet vermouth

2–3 dashes Angostura or Peychaud bitters

Homemade Luxardo Cherries

(see page 73 for cherry recipe)

In a large glass or cocktail shaker, add bourbon and sweet vermouth. Add a dash or two of bitters. Add ice and mix. Strain into a martini glass and add a homemade luxardo cherry.

NOTE: I like my Manhattan shaken to get it really cold and to break down small bits of the ice into the cocktail. Some people prefer it stirred. Just like bourbon, drink it the way you want to drink it!

Calling All
Bourbon Badasses

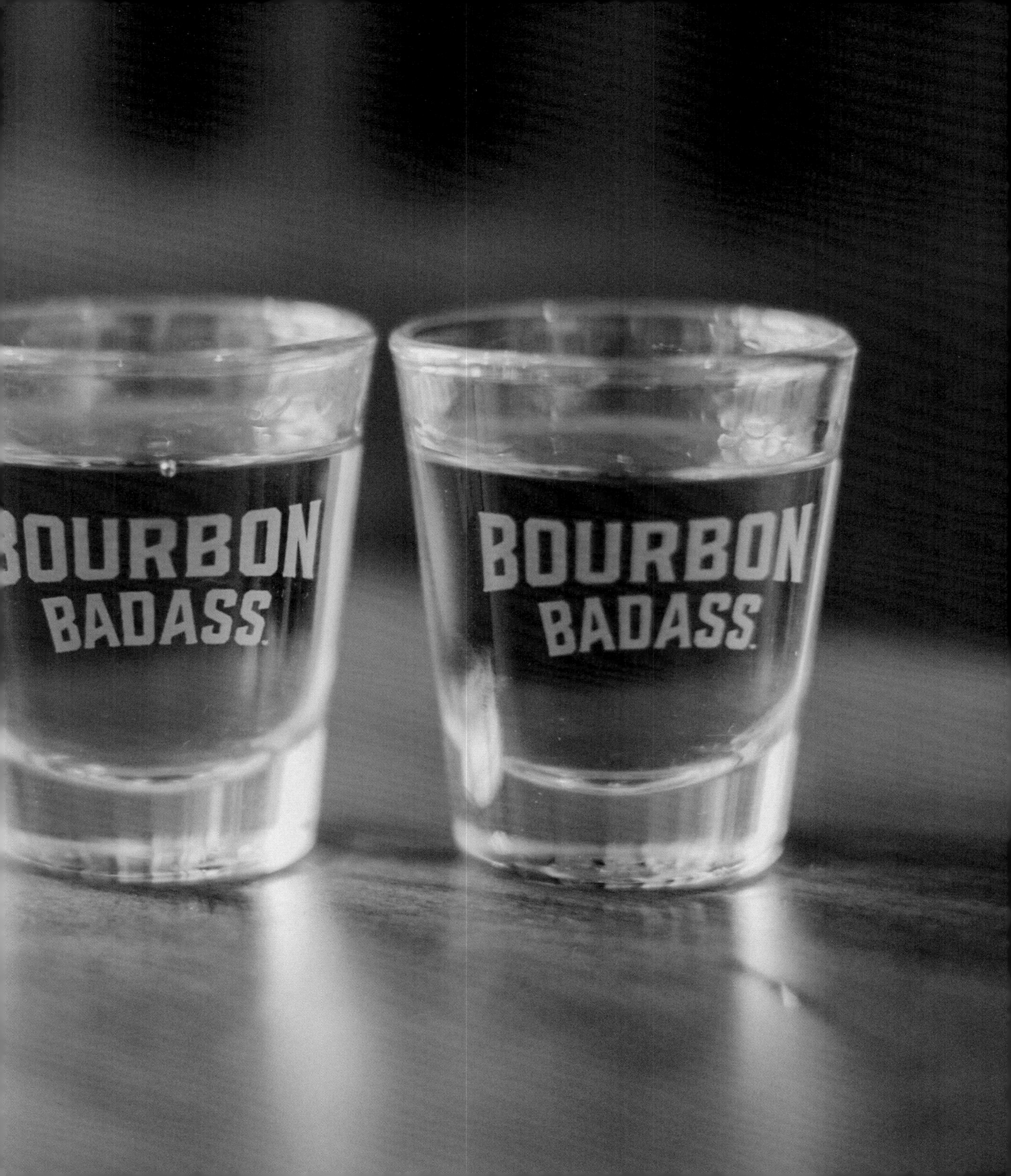
BOURBON
BADASS
BOURBON
BADASS

SIX | *Calling All Bourbon Badasses*

A good friend of mine relocated to Kentucky from Michigan. She had been trying for years to convince her mom and sister to try bourbon. Year after year they resisted until she finally convinced them to join her on a trip to the Maker's Mark distillery with the Whisky Chicks. The morning started out with scrumptious maple bacon doughnuts from a favorite bakery, Nord's, and a cup of Maker's Mark Kentucky Coffee. From the first taste they became intrigued, not believing that such a combination could be so delicious. Their bourbon journey began well, and they spent the rest of the day attentively listening and learning about the history of Maker's Mark and what makes it such a gem among the many Kentucky distilleries. They willingly dipped their finger into the bubbling mash bill to taste the sweetness of the distiller's "beer," while asking questions about the different factors that impact the flavor of bourbon. Before long they were seated in the front row of the tasting room, sampling the different selections in the Maker's Mark portfolio. They topped off their experience by dipping their very own bottles of Maker's Mark in the famous red sealing wax.

But the adventure didn't stop there. Upon leaving the distillery, they took their newfound knowledge to their local liquor store, where they picked up a sampling of bourbons, including Bulleit, Blanton's, and Basil Hayden's. Those are all delicious selections for the novice bourbon drinker. They put together their own tasting, noting the differences in flavors, mixing them with various ingredients to create their own cocktails—and now it's safe to call them passionate pursuers of all things bourbon. It's that simple. A whole world of bourbon-inspired fun awaits them.

Fast-forward a few months. My friend's sister was preparing for her first date after her nearly twenty-year marriage ended in divorce. She met a gentleman through an online dating service, and, needless to say, she was nervous. She had gone through

Kentucky Coffee

Ingredients:
1 part Maker's Mark bourbon
1 part cream liqueur
Splash of DeKuyper Hazelnut
 Liqueur
Hot, fresh coffee
Whipped cream for garnish

Pour Maker's Mark bourbon and cream liqueur into an Irish coffee glass. Add DeKuyper Hazelnut Liqueur, and fill the glass with hot coffee. Top off with a dollop of whipped cream.

quite a bit of change over the previous year and was just now in a place where she felt sure enough to venture into the dating world. She just had to get through this first one.

She arrived early to their prearranged meeting place. She casually sat at the bar and ordered a Blanton's on the rocks, her new favorite, and waited. Shortly afterward, her date arrived and introduced himself, asking what she was drinking. She proudly shared that she was drinking Blanton's bourbon on the rocks. His response was classic as he exclaimed, "Why, aren't you a badass!" In her mind she was thinking, "Why, yes, I am!" as a surge of confidence emboldened her.

Her confidence did not come from the bourbon itself, even though that may have helped a bit; it came from the knowledge she had gained about bourbon. During the first few ice-breaking minutes with her new friend, she shared a bit of what she had learned about bourbon, a drink many think of as exclusive to guys. She spoke assuredly about the reasons she preferred Blanton's over other bourbons, how she had tried different ones and settled on this as her first choice; she added that it can be difficult to find Blanton's in bars outside of Kentucky. Talk about a conversation starter!

Stories like this one are part of what has made this journey with the Whisky Chicks so fascinating and fulfilling. I have met women from all different walks of life and from different places in the world, ranging in age from twenty-one to ninety-four. All of them have a sense of curiosity and a desire to learn more about the world around them. They want to experience new things and are open to adventures that involve the senses. Coming together to share a glass of bourbon has created bonds between individuals that otherwise had very little in common. One of my favorite connections is between Joan and Maggie.

Joan is an amazing woman in her own right. Imagine a five-foot-tall white-haired, half-Irish and half-Jewish spitfire with a zest for life. She loves to share with anyone who will listen her thoughts on business, bourbon, politics, life, you name it. She pulls you into conversation with her intriguing point of view. She is originally from New York, where she started her career much like a character in *Mad Men*, working as a "girl Friday" for a marketing agency and eventually working her way up into positions traditionally held by men. During this time, her drink of choice was either Jack Daniel's Tennessee Whiskey or Wild Turkey. She has been through so much in her life, surviving divorce, breast cancer, major career changes, and business ownership. When you meet Joan, you meet someone with a huge heart and a passion for gab. She loves bourbon and wants to learn and experience all she can about America's native spirit.

Meet Maggie. Maggie is an accomplished writer who has published pieces in such online and print magazines as *Whisky Magazine*, the *Whiskey Wash*, and *Alcohol Professor*. She is the mother of two young boys. Her brown curly hair and retro style is reminiscent of the '50s. Her experiences with bourbon began a few years ago when she was working part-time at a local liquor store and had the honor of meeting master distiller Jim Rutledge. One night the store was hosting a tasting of Four Roses. She kept trying to make her way over to the tasting, but things were so busy she missed the whole thing. Disappointed, she went on break—and the next thing she knew, Jim Rutledge was standing there with samples in hand just for her. He was dismayed that she had been unable to be part of the evening. He went out of his way to make sure she was able to enjoy his handcrafted product. This was her "aha" moment. A new passion was discovered, and since that time Maggie has taken advantage of every opportunity to learn and write about bourbon, including sharing stories about groups like the Whisky Chicks. It was at a Whisky Chicks event that Joan and Maggie met.

Now, two years later, when you meet Maggie and Joan, you first think they may be mother and daughter, even though they look nothing alike. What you soon discover are two souls that must have been connected in a previous life. They are kindred spirits who now spend every Monday morning together discussing business strategies; they are even designing a line of bourbon-inspired jewelry together. Maggie has become the daughter Joan never had, and Joan has become a friend and source of inspiration for Maggie. They have a unique bond that can be so hard to find, and it all started with a glass of bourbon.

There are mothers and daughters, daughters and sons, and, my favorite, fathers and daughters who have come together to a Whisky Chicks event. We even had three generations from one family at a tasting. Bonding over a glass of bourbon can be a way to find common ground between very different individuals. And that can turn into a lifetime bond, sparking new discoveries in other areas of life. At every tasting we learn something new, find a new flavor, uncover some little-known bit of history or a technique that enhances the tasting experience. Exploring bourbon is a lifelong adventure full of stories, places, personalities, and people that always delight.

When Candace, another Whisky Chicks attendee, returned to Louisville after being away for years, she proclaimed her first year back as her "year of bourbon." Years later she is still exploring and now believes this may be a lifelong endeavor. Being from Kentucky, she began her journey with a mix of curiosity combined with fond childhood memories. She remembers her mom and dad enjoying an evening cocktail of bourbon and Sprite. She has spent the last few years exploring her own preferences, tasting a wide array of bourbons, visiting multiple distilleries, and connecting with others who share her passion. Somewhere along the way she asked her ninety-four-year-old mother, Helen, to join her on this journey. Helen is an inspiration to so many. Age has not slowed her down much; she can be found right there sitting alongside the twenty-somethings at our tastings, experiencing and learning new things about America's native spirit. She will try anything, but she has her own preferences and knows what she likes and what she doesn't like. Spending the day with her touring the Four Roses distillery will always be a highlight for me on my own personal journey. It made me realize that regardless of age, there is always something new to learn and experience. That day I declared I want to be like Helen when I grow up!

When Helen turned ninety-four, we plotted with her daughters to throw her a surprise birthday party. It was my husband, Fred, who came up with the theme of

Helen's ninety-fourth birthday celebration. *Photos by Christy Cates.*

"ninety-four years of bourbon." He pulled together seven different bourbons whose combined age was ninety-four. The lineup included Old Grand Dad Bonded (four years), Old Weller Antique Original 107 (seven years), Old Rip Van Winkle (ten years), Van Winkle Special Reserve (twelve years), Eagle Rare Antique Collection (seventeen years), Willett Family Estate Single Barrel (twenty-one years), and Pappy Van Winkle (twenty-three years).

One Whisky Chick, Nikki, has been married over twenty-five years to her high school sweetheart. When you meet Nikki, the first thing you notice is how vivacious and outgoing she is. She truly lights up a room. She is a natural-born extrovert and socialite who loves being around other people. She put her social life on hold for a few years to focus on her family, but as her son got older and began to strike out on his own, she started looking for new ways to connect with other women. At the invitation of a friend, she attended her first Whisky Chicks event. In her own words: "My usual adult beverage of choice is white wine. I had never had bourbon before that night. Not only did I learn interesting facts regarding bourbon, but I also met a diverse group of dynamic women! With each event, I am educated with new information about bourbon, while meeting intelligent, confident, friendly, laid-back, and classy individuals."

Now, a few years and several events later, Nikki has progressed from a bourbon novice to a true enthusiast. She feels confident at dinner or at a bar ordering her favorite small batch neat and sipping it throughout the evening. She is not afraid to try new things and is always the first to declare if a specific bourbon goes to the top of her list. As she puts it, "One qualifying characteristic of a straight bourbon is that it is aged for a minimum of two years. I am proud to say I have been a Whisky Chick for more than two years and just like fine bourbon, it just gets better every year."

Nikki Rhodes, Whisky Chicks member, at one of her first tasting events.

One of the most amazing parts of the bourbon industry is its sense of community. Even though the different distilleries represent competing brands, the collaboration and mutual support among them is something I have never seen in any other industry. If equipment breaks down and a necessary part is not available for days, the distillery down the street is more than willing to come to the rescue. They truly believe all boats rise with the tide, and over the years they have partnered to promote the bourbon industry as a whole. Nothing exemplifies this more than the 1996 fire at Heaven Hill Distillery.

It all started in Warehouse I. With winds blowing at seventy-five miles per hour, the fire quickly spread across the Heaven Hill campus, even traveling over a nearby creek. The blaze eventually destroyed several buildings, including seven warehouses and the original Heaven Hill distillery. At one point, the flames were said to be 350 feet high, streams of lit bourbon were flowing down the hillside like lava, and the inferno could be seen for miles. With ninety thousand barrels of bourbon destroyed that day, the future of Heaven Hill was at risk. But this is where the industry stepped in. Competing distilleries opened their doors to do contract distilling for Heaven Hill so they could continue to produce their family-owned products. Miraculously no one was killed that day and no one lost their job. Heaven Hill was able to recover from this disaster and continues to be one of the biggest producers of bourbon in the world, owning such brands as Evan Williams, Larceny, Elijah Craig, Bernheim, and Henry McKenna.

It was this sense of community that inspired the Whisky Chicks to incorporate a commitment to giving back as part of our mission. Around the same time that the Whisky Chicks was founded, a similar organization called the Bourbon Brotherhood was also founded. We joined forces to produce an annual fundraising event called the Bourbon Mixer. During the first three years, we were able to raise over $65,000 for two local charities. Held in August each year, the Bourbon Mixer brings together more than fifteen distilleries representing over fifty brands. It gives guests the opportunity to sample the bourbon, as well as to mix and mingle with bourbon celebs like

Buffalo Trace Bourbon Cream Root Beer Float

2 ounces Buffalo Trace Distillery
   Bourbon Cream
4 ounces root beer

Combine in glass and serve.
For extra richness, pour over a
scoop of vanilla ice cream.

master distillers, owners, and ambassadors. We encourage each distillery to prepare a unique cocktail for the evening that helps ease the novice bourbon drinker into the experience. We have had such concoctions as bourbon popsicles, bourbon cream root beer floats, and peach bourbon slushies.

Catherine Platz, whiskey brand ambassador, Brown-Forman.

It is through the Bourbon Mixer and other hosted events that I have had the opportunity to meet so many unbelievable women who work in the bourbon industry. Even though the industry has been traditionally male dominated, women continue to make their mark as master distillers, master tasters, brand ambassadors, and distillery owners. Each of them has a story to tell. They all share a passion for Kentucky bourbon and for guiding others on their journey, helping both men and women discover the best their spirits have to offer.

When you meet Catherine Platz (a.k.a. Cat) you first see a petite blonde-haired, sometimes purple-haired, fashion-forward young professional who is passionate about her job as whiskey brand ambassador for one of the world's largest spirits producers. Sometimes underestimated by her audience, she is just like Elle in *Legally Blonde*. She will blow you away with her knowledge about whiskey, especially Kentucky bourbon. I still remember the first time that Cat presented at a Whisky Chicks event. Up until then, I had made the same assumption that many people make in this business, that most of the whiskey brand representatives were men. I remember thinking she was totally badass when she showed up with her own (male) assistant, who was very quiet but dutifully helped her prepare for the evening's tasting, carrying boxes, setting up glasses, and hanging out in the back of the room waiting to respond should the need arise. He was one of only two men in the room that evening but did not seem at all uncomfortable. It was only later in the evening, when Cat introduced me to Aaron, that I realized he was not her assistant but was instead her longtime boyfriend. I remember thinking what an awesome guy he was, and the better I have gotten to know both of them over the years, the more I appreciate how it takes a strong man to be with an equally strong woman.

Cat represents several top brands, bringing them to life and creating memorable experiences with them. As a native of Nashville, Tennessee, her whiskey heritage is more Tennessee whiskey than Kentucky bourbon. Jack Daniel's was the brand she grew up knowing, and to this day a sip of Jack Daniel's Black Label will bring her back home. Cat started as a bartender in college and found there was good money to be made as a promo rep at trade shows and large events. She has flown all over the country representing everything from tablets and network routers to cars and sports drinks. As she is quick to point out, not all promo girls are just eye candy. You have to be intelligent and well versed in and informed about the product you are showcasing, especially when it comes to bourbon and whiskey. The average consumer is better informed than ever before. They ask tough questions, and you have to be prepared. They can be extremely loyal to their favorite brands—so loyal, in fact, that they have infamous brands tattooed all over their bodies. From what Cat tells me, it truly is ALL parts of the body and they LOVE to show them off. Ah, the glamorous life of a brand ambassador. Cat has truly earned her chops as a Bourbon Badass.

Fellow Bourbon Badass Megan Breier grew up in northern Kentucky. Her first memory of bourbon was sparked by her father, who loved making Maker's Mark Manhattans. She never really drank bourbon until she moved to Louisville to work for the uniquely famous 21c Museum Hotel. *Condé*

Megan Brier.

Colleen Thomas, bourbon ambassador for the Kentucky Distillers' Association.

Nast Traveler magazine has listed 21c numerous times as one of the top ten hotels in the world. It is a boutique Louisville hotel that is known for its contemporary art museum, its award-winning restaurant, and its fabulous bar, which has an extensive bourbon collection. As the event manager, Megan quickly learned how important bourbon was to the heritage of Louisville. Even in 2008, a few years before the bourbon boom really began, 21c took learning about bourbon seriously and invested in expanding the staff's knowledge. They championed renowned author and bourbon authority Bernie Lubbers to do a training course for their entire staff. Bernie, who now works for Heaven Hill, was part of the Jim Beam brand at the time. He introduced Megan to the Jim Beam small batch collection. From there she fell in love with the stories, the history, and the bourbon itself.

Megan used her recently discovered passion and knowledge to create one-of-a-kind experiences at 21c that were geared toward education and, for the first time, targeted the female consumer. She did her job so well she was eventually recruited away to join Jim Beam as their brand ambassador for Kentucky. Megan now spreads the joy of bourbon to the West Coast as the bourbon ambassador for California, Nevada, Oregon, and Washington State. She loves that no matter where she is or who she meets, when she shares what she does, people get excited and want to learn more.

Colleen Thomas is another Bourbon Badass who has helped many craft distillers get started on their journey to creating their own spirit. Fairly common to the industry, hers is a story more about destiny and fate than intentional planning. After being a stay-at-home mom, Colleen took her first step back into the workforce by doing marketing consulting for Flavorman, which is recognized as one of the leading experts in the development of flavors for beverages, including distilled spirits. After being on the job for just a few short months, the owner, Dave Defoe, charged Colleen, Colin Blake, and Kevin Hall with developing a distillery education center. It was later named the Distilled Spirits Epicenter.

With the increasing interest in craft distilling, Dave saw a need for quality education and wanted to offer the industry something that had never been done before: a full-immersion course on how to open, operate, and run a distillery. The team, including Colleen, Colin, and Kevin, brought in experts to help build the curriculum, put together a working still, and create the marketing to recruit students. Colleen herself underwent a deep immersion into everything from learning the mechanics of running a still to study-ing the chemical reactions that take place as part of the distillation process to becoming an expert on local bourbon lore. The end result was the creation of Moonshine University, where visitors learn how to build, open, and run their own distilleries. There's also the fully equipped Grease Monkey Distillery, which when not in use for classes is available to develop mash bills, create prototype batches, and experiment with processing or full-run productions.

Colleen was recruited away by the Kentucky Distillers' Association to be their bour-bon ambassador. Her job is to share Kentucky's rich heritage in spirits with the rest of the world. She is the perfect person for the job given that she coauthored the curriculum used today by Moonshine University to develop the first industry-endorsed bourbon certification program, the Stave & Thief Society Executive Bourbon Steward program. This premier training and education program was established to promote and uphold bourbon's unique and distinguished culture by preparing those in the hospitality industry to deliver on the promise of the authentic bourbon experience. As a certified executive bourbon steward, I can attest to the quality and thoroughness of the training provided. When you see the Stave & Thief Society seal posted by an establishment, you can be con-fident that the folks serving have received the proper bourbon education. In fact, Colin, the current director of spirits education for Moonshine University, has become another bourbon mentor and a guide along my bourbon journey.

Moonshine University has been the impetus for many craft distillers from all over the country to open their doors. These establishments include Kentucky Peerless Distilling

Future Rock Star of Bourbon

When I first met Caleb Kilburn, it was on a tour of one of Louisville's newest distilleries, Kentucky Peerless Distilling Company. I knew from the moment I met him that he was destined to one day be a rock star of bourbon. His friendly, approachable demeanor was magnetic, and when he talked about his craft, you could see the spark in his eyes. When we met, he was only twenty-three years old, but he spoke like someone who had been in the industry since birth. And yet he hadn't grown up in this industry. It wasn't part of his pedigree. They say in this industry that most distillers are either passionate about the science or the artistry. Caleb is passionate about both.

Caleb grew up in a small town in eastern Kentucky called Salt Lick, population 310. His family owned a small dairy farm with fifty head of cattle, and he learned from day one the importance of hard work and ingenuity. He was surrounded by individuals who imparted to him strong core values, an incredible work ethic, and a fervent belief that if you have a problem, you own it and fix it. No excuses. As an only child and the only grandchild for the first eleven years of his life, he was reminded on a daily basis that he was fortunate but not privileged.

When he tells the story of his grandfather Poppy, you quickly understand how this young man has accomplished so much in his short life. Two years before Caleb was born, Poppy and Caleb's dad were tending cattle and Poppy got caught up in one of the tractors. When he was able to free himself from the tractor, all he had left on was one boot and his underwear. The doctors said that if it hadn't been one of the coldest days of the year, he would have died right there. Instead, he survived, but the accident left him with his right arm removed and a severely injured leg that the doctors recommended be amputated, though the family refused. The doctors said he would never walk again, but a few years later not only could he walk, he could run.

Caleb grew up watching Poppy constantly overcome challenges on the farm that came with having only one arm. Something as simple as putting a tarp over his truck bed was difficult, so Poppy invented a system of ropes and pulleys to make it easier. He somehow figured out how to use a posthole digger with one arm and designed vises and drills that made farm duties possible. As Caleb grew up, he was always at Poppy's side, and as he puts it, he became his grandfather's right hand. He learned that there is no obstacle you cannot overcome.

His upbringing in an atmosphere of ingenuity and can-do attitude has helped make Caleb successful in his first run as head distiller. Caleb always had an interest in chemistry, biology, and physics. When he was in college at Morehead State University, he was challenged to choose between the three disciplines. He loves to learn, and when he was introduced to distilling, he realized how immensely complicated it was, which he found fascinating. He began to go on distillery tours and would always hang back and ask the tour guide or the distiller if he could come back and shadow them for a day. Some said yes and some just gave him funny looks.

It was his girlfriend, Paige, who heard a piece on NPR about a five-day distiller course. It changed Caleb's destiny. Just barely twenty-one years old, he knew he had to go. Before enrolling, he was invited to tour the facility, and he became enamored with the in-house 250-gallon pot still. He totally geeked out on the equipment, the process, the science, and the art of making spirits. It was in this five-day course that he met his future mentors. Caleb credits his success to the folks at Moonshine University, including Kevin Hall, Colleen Thomas, Colin Blake, and longtime industry experts Pete Kamer (retired distillery engineer for Barton Brands) and Rob Sherman (fourth-generation owner of Vendome Copper). This group of advocates introduced Caleb to Kentucky Peerless Distilling Company owners Corky and Carson Taylor.

When Caleb first met Corky and Carson, the distillery building still had a dirt floor and the company was closer to a dream than reality. Caleb's career at Peerless began the summer before his last year in college. He started out sawing, stacking lumber, and pulling nails. After a few weeks he graduated to shoveling gravel. Over time different production-related tasks started to come up. The team soon discovered that Caleb was not only the youngest worker in the building but also the only one on the team literate in pipe fittings and mechanical systems. His experience on the dairy farm served him well. He soon became involved in the installation of steam lines and chilled-water lines, and he eventually oversaw the installation of different equipment in the distillery.

When it came to the design of the distillery, he took it upon himself to create an eleven-page list of every valve and their associated operating procedures. For him it was like playing with Legos, and he was determined to partner with Corky and Carson to create a cutting-edge, innovative distillery that produced the best juice in the business. As a result, the Kentucky Peerless distillery is recognized as one of the most technologically advanced craft distilleries in the world and produces some of the best tasting ryes that leading whiskey experts like Mike Veach have ever had. Their bourbon is still aging, but I have no doubt it will be outstanding.

I can say I knew him before he became the rock star of the spirits industry that he is destined to become. Caleb Kilburn is a Bourbon Badass!

Company, Jeptha Creed, and Dueling Grounds in Kentucky; Old Forge in Tennessee; Call Family and Copper Barrel in North Carolina; Alchemy in Arcata, California; Dry Hills in Bozeman, Montana; and 10th Mountain Whiskey & Spirit Company in Vail, Colorado. They have provided a breakthrough platform for those who dream of being part of the industry.

Jane Thomas Bowie grew up in a dry town in Kentucky. After graduating from college, instead of pursuing a career, she made the choice—much to her parents' dismay—to travel around Europe. She

Jane Thomas Bowie, head of innovation at Maker's Mark.

grabbed her backpack and headed off to London, where she worked behind the bar pulling pints until her visa ran out six months later. She thought her traveling adventures were over until a friend mentioned she was teaching English as a second language in Japan. Jane applied for the job and moved there for two years. She was in her early twenties at the time, and it was the perfect job for this native Kentucky girl.

When people discovered she was from Kentucky, they always wanted to know if she ate Kentucky Fried Chicken and drank Kentucky bourbon. Although people in Japan were obsessed with Colonel Sanders, Jane opted to become an expert on bourbon instead of KFC. There were several whiskey bars that carried extensive collections of Kentucky bourbon. A bar could carry forty to fifty different types of bourbon, and regardless of the selection they were all the same price. A glass of Blanton's Small Batch ($60 a bottle) cost the same price as one of Kentucky Tavern ($10 a bottle). Jane's self-taught bourbon journey began in the land of the rising sun.

After two years, it was time for Jane to move back to Kentucky. Her mom had moved to Louisville, so she joined her there and started working at the Seelbach Hotel. After

being home a few months, Jane felt the itch to travel again and started planning a move to New Zealand as a rafting guide. Her parents expressed their concern and suggested it was time for Jane to get her act together and perhaps settle on a career. They even began to peruse the local help wanted ads to see if they could find something Jane would enjoy. That is when her mom stumbled across an ad for a Maker's Mark event coordinator. Jane's initial reaction was mixed. She loved the idea of working for Maker's Mark but wasn't as thrilled by the idea of being an event coordinator. In response to the ad, Jane took the bold step of drafting a letter, explaining that she did not really want the job advertised but would love to utilize her international experience and love of all things Kentucky to share Maker's Mark with the world.

As they sometimes say, timing is everything. The hiring manager had just been tasked with coming up with a plan to grow Maker's Mark internationally. As luck would have it, Jane did not get the job for event coordinator but instead became the first Maker's Mark international brand ambassador. She spent the next four years traveling to nine different countries, eventually settling in London. When she moved back to Kentucky again, she was ecstatic to join the team on the ground in Loretto, Kentucky. Even through significant growth and its purchase by Beam Suntory, Maker's Mark has continued to hold on to its entrepreneurial spirit and family-centric culture, making it a place that feels like home.

From what I have experienced over the past few years, this feeling of family and home is a common thread that carries through the entire bourbon industry. It's more than selling whiskey. It's about history, innovation, growth, and a desire to share a product everyone involved takes pride in. I believe that's why an organization like the Whisky Chicks, an event like a bourbon tasting, or even a homespun bourbon-inspired dinner can and does change lives. I've met so many interesting people, some of whom are now lifelong friends. I've seen how passion and dedication to a craft can ignite conversation and new discoveries. I've even seen diverse individuals and competing businesses come together for a good cause, making our community better. Who knew that a glass of bourbon had such power? For me, Kentucky bourbon is more than a nice brown drink. It evokes good times, good people, and good memories. A sip can transport me back down Memory Lane. I invite you to walk with me down that welcoming path and begin your own bourbon journey to becoming a Bourbon Badass.

Acknowledgments

There are too many incredible Whisky Chicks and Bourbon Badasses to list by name. Thank you to everyone who believed in the vision of the Whisky Chicks and to those who took the time to impart and share their knowledge and experience with me.

To Erin Trimble, who is such a talented photographer, thank you for capturing the beauty of the bourbon and all the people who love it. Special thanks to Becca Probus, who was part of hatching the original idea for Whisky Chicks.

To my wonderful family, including my three siblings, Rob, Mike, and Anna, you have been there for me my entire life. Rob, thank you for marrying your incredible and amazing wife. Chandra, without you and your incredible editing skills, I am not sure this book would have ever made it to print.

To my dad, even though you are not physically here with us anymore, your spirit lives on every time I host a Whisky Chicks party. You taught me how to make people feel comfortable, no matter the circumstances. From your passing, I learned the importance of being mindful of the legacy we leave behind and that the greatest gift you can give yourself is to pay it forward.

To my two sons, you are the light of my life. Thanks so much for your patience and for keeping Mommy grounded through this process.

Linda Ruffenach, the founder of the Whisky Chicks, believes there is not a right way or wrong way to drink bourbon. In fact, she believes that everyone's journey is different and that for many, taking the leap from wine to whiskey can be incredibly intimidating. Her objective? Make it easy to take your first step.

Born and raised in Louisville, Kentucky, she takes pride in creating experiences that make learning about Kentucky bourbon approachable, fun, and informative. She created the Whisky Chicks in 2014 out of a desire to meet other women who had nothing to do with her job, spouse, or kids. Since then she has partnered with top international brands to create over fifty unique experiences and has helped over one thousand men and women on their journey to bourbon enlightenment.

She has been described as a kind of no-nonsense, direct, warm southern woman who will go out of her way to make sure everyone around her feels comfortable. She loves to play hostess and knows how to throw a hell of a party. Sharing a glass of bourbon and learning about America's native spirit can be the great common denominator for bringing people together. What she has created is a community of women (and a few men) ranging in age from twenty-one to ninety-four who support, inspire, and empower each other.

ACQUIRING EDITOR
Ashley Runyon

PROJECT MANAGER
Rachel Rosolina

BOOK & COVER DESIGNER
Jennifer L. Witzke